THE KU KLUX KLAN

IN

SOUTH DAKOTA

THE KU KLUX KLAN
IN
SOUTH DAKOTA

ARLEY KENNETH FADNESS

THE
History
PRESS

Published by The History Press
Charleston, SC
www.historypress.com

First published 2024

Manufactured in the United States

ISBN 9781467154246

Library of Congress Control Number: 2022951601

CONTENTS

CONTENTS

PREFACE

History could make a stone weep
—Gilead, *by Marilynne Robinson*

I stood in line at Perebom's restaurant in Webster, South Dakota, a few years ago, waiting my turn to purchase two autographed books by local author Bob Bartos. Bob scribbled his name, pocketed my money and handed me two soft-bound books: *Memories of the Millennium* and *Memories of the Millennium II.*

Bob had been a weekly columnist for the *Reporter and Farmer* newspaper for many years and had now gathered prized stories from the columns and plunked them into two newsy, folksy books.

Later, settled comfortably in my easy chair, I began reading *Memories of the Millennium II.* Oh, what fun! Jackrabbit hunting, fishing, the origins of the Lawrence Welk band, livery barns and lazy days at the lake. Fifty stories of pastoral scenes, humor and romance—many reflections of my boyhood on the farm in Day County, South Dakota. But then came chapter 51!

"The Ku Klux Klan gathers in large numbers and burns three crosses in Webster, South Dakota!"[1]

As I read in disbelief, I blurted, "Could it be? Couldn't be! Can't be! My hometown!"

I was born in Webster, South Dakota. Lived and raised among the good, God-fearing citizens of Day County. The Ku Klux Klan in my hometown? Sure enough. I read on.

Still quoting from his published columns in the *Reporter and Farmer*, Bob reiterated:

April 23, 1925—A speaker for the Ku Klux Klan held forth at the opera house Monday evening to a good sized crowd.

Tuesday night at about 11 o'clock a fiery cross was burned on the lower end of Main Street. It was a large cross and illuminated that section of town for quite a time....A second cross was burned Wednesday night, on the north end of main street.[2]

Another entry:

July 16, 1925—Thousands see KKK meeting. Many states represented in gathering to witness session of Klan. The largest crowd which ever gathered in Webster attended the demonstration of the Ku Klux Klan on the hill east of the city Monday evening. There was no way to check the number of cars or people who attended but it is generally conceded that in the neighborhood of 2,000 automobiles were present, which would mean at least 5,000 people. In the string of cars were noticed number plates representing many different states and most counties of South Dakota sent representatives.[3]

The speaker of the evening held a large crowd in front of the platform for more than an hour and received good attention....His topic was Americanism and covered thoroughly many things every citizen should bear in mind. Perhaps the greatest attraction for visitors was the display of fireworks and burning of crosses. The display of fireworks, while not particularly large, was very beautiful and burning three K's and three crosses presented a spectacular sight against the dark sky about midnight.[4]

Duane Anderson, curator of the Webster Museum of Wildlife and Science and Industry, informed me on one of my visits to Webster that the scars in the prairie grasses of those three KKKs and the three crosses are still visible on that east hill just outside of town.

Bob Bartos, quoting further from the columns he wrote for the *Reporter and Farmer*, illustrated the close connections between the Ku Klux Klan and Protestant churches in America—and specifically in Webster, South Dakota.

He wrote that on September 10, 1925,

> *The Methodist Episcopal Church Sunday evening was attended by about 25 members of the Ku Klux Klan in full regalia.*
> *The address by Rev. Bullock, "100 percent American, who are they?" was an able effort and much appreciated by the large audience. Appropriate music added much to a very fine program.*[5]

So began a quest and the genesis for this book. Compelled to research and find out more about one shady chapter in my past, a clear purpose evolved. The purpose would evolve into a simple attempt to "strengthen our democracy" by learning the follies of the Ku Klux Klan in the Rushmore State and compare them to the amendments to our Constitution.

I pounced on primary sources such as the essays by former state historian Ken Stewart, Professor Charles Rambow and William Harwood.

I mined a lode of lectures, archival newspaper articles, photos and pamphlets on the subject of the Ku Klux Klan in South Dakota. I interviewed Ken, Chuck, numerous librarians, editors, museum curators and ordinary citizens who carried Klan stories and remembrances of past generational family members and neighbors.

I found no specific book dedicated to exposing the presence and activities of the Ku Klux Klan, "smack dab" in the middle of the beautiful Rushmore State of South Dakota—so I yield to you this humble script.

History aficionados! For your enlightenment, trepidation, insight and hopefully a tad of enjoyment—read on.

ACKNOWLEDGEMENTS

I gratefully give credit to the late Bob Bartos from Webster, South Dakota, who launched me into this surprising and amazing orbital project. Through my personal friendship with Bob and then reading his book *Memories of Millennium II*, I discovered a shadowy chapter in my history and in my state that I never knew a lick about.

I am warmed by the generosity and friendship of Charles Rambow, who agreed to an unforgettable interview at his home, one sunny afternoon, in Rapid City. As Charles Rambow talked about his experiences, lectures and findings, he shared multiple Ku Klux Klan artifacts with me that he had gathered from his family, neighbors and the Black Hills area. Rambow's master's thesis on the Ku Klux Klan, "The Ku Klux Klan in the 1920's: A Concentration on the Black Hills," proved invaluable in my research. His artifacts include a tiny KKK bible; a charter for the Mile Hi Klan in Lead/Sturgis; photos of Klan gatherings in a barn hayloft in downtown Sturgis and the KKK funeral for M.M. Baird on May 30, 1926; Charles grandfather's KKK robe and hood; a KKK coin, creed and assorted KKK memorabilia.

"The Ku Klux Klan in South Dakota," a paper presented at the Dakota History Conference in Madison in 1971 by Kenneth Stewart, was an eye-opener. Stewart, former archival staff at the South Dakota State Historical Society, collected KKK articles in 1920s newspapers that spotlighted KKK activities and mayhem in South Dakota.

I valued conversations with Christine Erickson, associate professor at Indiana University–Purdue University, Fort Wayne, whose research and plans for a book on the Ku Klux Klan in Montana is hopefully forthcoming.

Longtime friend the Center for Western Studies at Augustana University provided a speaking venue for me on the topic of the Ku Klux Klan in South Dakota. Also, at a prior Dakota Conference year at the Center for Western Studies my imagination was sparked by Professor Anita Gaul from the University of Minnesota–Worthington who spoke on the movement and activities of the Ku Klux Klan in southwestern Minnesota. A paper by William L. Harwood titled "The Ku Klux Klan In Grand Forks, North Dakota" recounted the robust and illustrious Reverend F. Halsey Ambrose, who influenced all levels of government in Grand Forks, North Dakota, and beyond by his powerful anti-Catholic preaching. I used the resources of the South Dakota State Historical Society and the University of North Dakota special collections archives as well as several South Dakota newspaper archives and especially the gracious help at the Mitchell Public Library in Mitchell.

Thanks to local historian Jim Carlson for a copy of the application request to the Sioux Falls mayoral office by the KKK for a free public meeting. Thanks to Robert Kolbe for a KKK "Klan in Action" article artifact; Donna Weiland of Mitchell for the Corn Palace photograph; Tony Meager of Prescott, Arizona; for the original image of the Congregational Church in Beresford; and Sharon Schnabel from Yankton about her mother bootlegger, Leona Pietz. Thanks to staff at the Canton Public Library.

DEMOCRACY AND THE PRINCIPLES OF EQUALITY TESTED

In 1883, the poet Emma Lazarus wrote the classic sonnet "The New Colossus." Lines from "The New Colossus," chiseled into stone, now appear on the gray pedestal of the Statue of Liberty in the New York Harbor.

The lines plead,
"Give me your tired, your poor, your huddled masses yearning to breathe free,
The Wretched refuse of your teeming shore;
Send these, the Homeless, Tempest-tost to me,
I Lift my lamp beside the Golden Door."[6]

And did they breathe free, those huddled masses, stepping off ocean liners and onto American soil.

It is estimated that between 1892 and 1924, twelve million immigrants sailed into the ports of New York and New Jersey and through that Golden Door.

Their first sight—the statue, *Lady Liberty*—holding the torch of freedom and saying welcome.

Very quickly, once settled, the huddled masses began participating in a democratic form of governing unlike anything they had experienced or could imagine.

The immigrant masses began seeking and embracing the soul-glowing dream of "We hold these truths to be self-evident, that all men are created equal, that they are endowed by their Creator with certain unalienable Rights, that among these are Life, Liberty and the pursuit of Happiness."

They would learn and embrace the ideal that democracy thrives when a community organizes its self-governance around the full participation, on an equal basis, of all the members of the community.

One group, however, in the history of the United States, did not fully embrace this true democratic ideal.

Under the cloak of 100 percent Americanism, while heralding and legitimizing segments of the Protestant religion, they hoodwinked much of the populace to follow their tenets and agenda.

I speak of the shady history of the Ku Klux Klan in America from 1915 to 1930. My focus and rationale in this book is to shine a spotlight on the forgotten and/or ignored history of the Ku Klux Klan's odious incursions into the Rushmore State.

Though the historicity may be in doubt, it is purported that when English soldier and statesman Oliver Cromwell sat for his portrait by Sir Peter Lely, he said, "Paint me as I am, warts and all." This is the legacy of a true and complete history. It will tell all, warts and all—the good, the bad and the ugly.

Throughout eight grades of country school, I was taught the good and the noble. We championed the Puritans and Pilgrims' quest for religious freedom. We reverently gazed on the portraits of Abraham Lincoln and George Washington prominently hung at the front of the schoolroom. We were taught all about Honest Abe walking miles to get a book and splitting rails. We were taught the myth of George Washington cutting down the cherry tree and saying to his father, "Father I cannot lie. I cut down the cherry tree."

We students marveled at the courage and perseverance of General Washington at Valley Forge and his fearless leadership crossing the dangerous Potomac in the Revolution and winning the war. We practically elevated Lincoln and Washington to the pantheon of immortals—Abraham, Jesus, Confucius, Aristotle and Moses. We hoisted the flag in our schoolyard each day and recited the Pledge of Allegiance. This teaching and patriotic ritual enabled and encouraged us to love America and appreciate and celebrate our freedoms. The history we learned saw America through rose-colored glasses.

Neither in grade school nor in high school at Augustana Academy at Canton did I ever learn about one specific tragic piece of Native American history. Two miles east of my high school in Canton lay the former site of the Hiawatha Indian Insane Asylum with its almost lost and forgotten cemetery of inmates. The Asylum for Insane Indians opened in 1902 as the second federally funded mental asylum in the United States. Patients were sent there for not only mental but also physical illnesses such as tuberculosis, epilepsy and various social maladies. "Idiotic" and incorrigible patients were sequestered there. It became a place of staggering misery and suffering. See Carla Joinson's book *Vanished in Hiawatha: The Story of the Canton Asylum for Insane Indians* for more.

I was taught nothing about the tragedies of the federal boarding schools whisking away children from their families and tribes. Nothing about Wounded Knee, the Trail of Tears, broken treaties or the warts and flaws of our historical heroes or the presence of the Ku Klux Klan in the Rushmore State. I was taught, with good intentions, a sanitized version of local history. Now I and many educators are beginning to realize selective history obscures and obfuscates the true facts. Knowing the dark stories of American history would not have lessened my patriotism or diminished my pride in my country. It would have celebrated truth in its fullness.

Larry L. Rasmussen's recollections, published in *The Planet You Inherit: Letters to My Grandchildren when Uncertainty Is a Sure Thing*, mirrors my own experience:

> *My entire world at your age…was Petersburg, Minnesota, a village of fifty hearts on the west branch of the Des Moines River.…This is a community where neither African Americans nor Native Americans were ever seen. When we learned Minnesota history in the sixth grade, we were*

Hiawatha Indian Insane Asylum, which became a dumping ground for inconvenient Indians in the nineteenth and early twentieth centuries. *South Dakota State Archives.*

not taught that Indigenous nations were still living in "our" Minnesota.
Even though thousands of Indian names of counties, towns, lakes, and
the state itself peppered themselves everywhere. (Minnesota is Dakota for
"where the water is so clear it reflects the sky.") Nor do I recall learning that
the largest public lynching in all of American history took place ninety miles
from Petersburg in Mankato, Minnesota, on the second day of Christmas,
1862. Thirty-eight Dakota warriors mounted the platform singing their
haunting Christian hymn, "Great Spirit of God."

The absence of Native Americans and Africans Americans from our
textbooks didn't deter tidbits that created toxic stories, however I remember
talent shows too. One year, maybe more, Dad and his best friend wore
Blackface in minstrel fashion and did their best at Black speech, jokes, and
a jig to the songs of Al Jolson. "Mammy, how I love ya, how I love ya, my
dear ol' mammy"…

And Dad and Loren were as kind and considerate as any men you'd meet.
Which is to say that good people are sometimes captive to terrible ideas. One
of evil's charming guises is innocence. This Innocence is the crime.[7]

It is becoming clearer and clearer that vibrant democracy thrives when the unvarnished truth is told. Progress is presently being made to correct one great omission in the teaching of South Dakota history—that is, to recover the Native American presence, history, life, language, culture and contributions to human society.

A second great omission, pleading for more attention, is to tell the unsavory presence and influence of the Ku Klux Klan in South Dakota society in the 1920s—and its chilling presence today.

When the full story, for example, of the construction, the symbolism and existence of Mount Rushmore is revealed, both its glory and its flaws, a balanced view of history can be celebrated.

Living in Custer, South Dakota, for twenty years, minutes away from the famous mountain and the four presidential busts, I thought I heard the full story. I joined with locals and thousands of tourists to behold the amazing monument, also called the *Shrine of Democracy*, many, many times. We the public offered unrestrained praise to the glory of freedom, liberty and the pursuit of happiness. The majesty of the four presidents is breathtaking. The artistry, mechanization and genius of sculptor Gutzon Borglum is beyond imagination.

But enter author Jesse Larner in his book *Mount Rushmore: An Icon Reconsidered*, in which he recounts one of his visits to Mount Rushmore:

Mount Rushmore, near Keystone, South Dakota, blasted and sculpted out of granite batholite into the likenesses of Presidents Washington, Jefferson, Lincoln and Roosevelt by Gutzon and Lincoln Borglum from 1927 to 1941. *Public domain.*

National Park Service rangers give a short orientation talk at the Sculptor's Studio, part of the Rushmore Complex, where Borglum's models, and explanation of his plans and various artifacts from the drilling and blasting are on display. When I saw this presentation, a clean cut ranger from Nebraska told the story of Doane Robinson's original idea and praised the political skills of Senator Peter Norbeck and Congressman William Williamson in getting Rushmore legislation passed. He spends some time on Borglum's vision, genius, and persistence....I wanted to know what this young Ranger thought of Borglum's ideas about white supremacy. How compatible could these ideas be with a modern evaluation of patriotism? After the ranger had finished his presentation, I asked him whether a discussion of Borglum and Rushmore was complete without mentioning Borglum's ties to the Ku Klux Klan. He spoke uncomfortably, "Well, I heard that he had some Klan connections."

I asked him more directly, whether Borglum's white supremacy should influence how we think about the meaning of Rushmore today; after all, so much else about the monument is associated with his personality. He gave a crisp and clear response. "I don't think that anything that Borglum may have thought or done personally has any relevance to Mount Rushmore as a national memorial. The meaning of Mount Rushmore is to honor these four presidents, our leaders."[8]

The full untold story is that the sculptor, Gutzon Borglum, stood firm in his conviction of the superiority of the Nordic European "race" and in defense of its destiny as the great civilizing influence in the world.

Among the history lessons I missed, besides the Hiawatha Indian Insane Asylum site and its existence two miles from my school, I missed knowing about the primary beliefs and practices of the Ku Klux Klan in my home community. I missed realizing the KKK was a group and a movement that touted white supremacy over all other races. The claim for 100 percent Americanism or "America First" conveniently overlooked the Fourteenth Amendment to the U.S. Constitution, which claims:

All persons born or naturalized in the United States and subject to the jurisdiction thereof, are citizens of the United States and of the State wherein they reside.....No State shall make or enforce any law which shall abridge the privilege or immunities of citizens of the United States nor shall any state deprive any person of life, liberty or property without due process of law.[9]

Would this knowledge have lessened my admiration for America? Would knowing that racism has been and is a plague since the founding of the United States destroy my faith in America, or would this knowledge help me work "for the freedoms and liberty for all" more diligently?

1

THE MURDER OF FATHER ARTHUR BARTHOLOMEW BELKNAP

One of the strongest tenets of the Ku Klux Klan in the 1920s was the belief that any allegiance to Catholicism was in reality a superior commitment to the pope in Rome. This belief overshadowed and corrupted citizens' commitment to the Constitution of the United States. The pope in Rome, Klan members spouted, had designs on infiltrating America and eventually become so powerful the pope would rule, if not physically, at least by capturing the hearts and minds of the populace. Therefore, any allegiance to Rome was anti-American.

It was around 3:00 a.m. on Wednesday, October 25, 1921, when local priest Father Arthur Belknap answered the knock on his rectory door in Lead, South Dakota. Three times before Father Belknap had been awakened in the night asking for pastoral care. But each time the odd disturbances had ended up a dead end. No one needing prayer, anointing of the sick or last rites known as the sacrament of Extreme Unction was found. Would this call for help be simply another false alarm?

The man knocking on the rectory door asked for pastoral care for someone at an address near Poorman Gulch where the Roundhouse Restaurant is located today in Lead. The rectory was situated at 141 Siever Street, which is the same location where St. Patrick's Church presently sits.

Anyone needing pastoral care was easily drawn like a magnet to seek out Father Belknap. "Father Belknap was a well-known figure about town...not only in the Lead/Deadwood area but also in much of the

Father Arthur Bartholomew Belknap.
Courtesy of the Rapid City Catholic Diocese.

northern Black Hills, having served as priest in the Belle Fourche, Vale and Spearfish communities."[10]

"The priest carried a 'triple threat' of characteristics that endeared him to Catholics and non-Catholics throughout the region. He was well-educated. He had an engaging personality. He was active in leading reform efforts in the Lead community."[11]

Father Belknap had gone on a mission in Lead. Perceptively, he saw some of the young miners spending their leisure time in Deadwood playing cards and engaging in dubious unhealthy activities at night. The miners were setting a poor example for the impressionable teens living in Lead and surrounding areas.

To begin to make social changes, Bishop John J. Lawler allowed and supported Father Belknap to lobby for his parishioners to have Sundays off from working in the mines. Homestake Gold Mine, founded in 1877, was the major employer at the time. The mine officials resented Belknap's proposal.

They complained that Sundays off might put into the miners' minds that there might be a higher priority than getting to work.

In general, Lead was not a Catholic-friendly community in 1921. The Catholic populace was told there was no place for a separate Catholic high school in town, despite Bishop Lawler's efforts to create one. There was a Catholic elementary school and hospital. A cloister of nuns ministered in both institutions; however, they were segregated from the rest of the Lead community.[12]

Father Arthur Belknap was an exception to the segregated status. His pastoral reputation drew people to him. Folks of all faiths respected and associated with him.

Although it was never stated publicly, there was fear that Father Belknap would reach celebrity status and garner even greater public support for his mission. Shortly before October 21, Father Belknap was busy raising money for a community center. The center would be a place for youth—all young people in the Lead area.[13]

Powerful men in the community took note. Mine officials, clergy, business leaders, anti-Catholic Masons and the Ku Klux Klan saw this center as a recruitment center to proselyte youth to Catholic membership. They were wrong. Father Belknap's vision saw his ministry as embracing the whole community for good.

When Father Belknap opened the rectory door that October night, the man knocking said there was need for a sick call at an address near Poorman Gulch. Father Belknap dressed, gathered his pastoral communion kit and went to fetch his car since Poorman Gulch was not only uphill on the mountain but also across town, and it seemed the call for help was urgent. Time was of the essence. He went into his garage, and the car would not start. The ignition refused to work. No wonder—it was jammed because the ignition had been smashed by a hammer prior to the knock on the rectory door.

So Father Belknap and the stranger set out on foot for Poorman Gulch. Would this be a fourth false alarm? One of the other times, Father Belknap's dedication took him a whole night of looking for a bogus address. He eventually gave up at daylight.

As Belknap and the stranger escort walked, they met a certain Arthur Miller, a mine worker who was going home from a shift. Miller pointed the two toward the address and went on his way.

Shortly after that brief exchange, it happened. Belknap's escort dropped back a few paces and allowed Father Belknap to walk ahead of him. The man pulled out a hammer and struck the priest in the back of the head. The priest was dazed. He staggered a few steps but stayed on his feet. Then the man pulled out a pistol and fired. Four or five .45-caliber bullets struck him. One pierced his heart as he fell to the ground.

The well-loved priest was dead.

On October 26, 1921, the *Lead Daily Call* headline read:

Father Belknap Cruelly Murdered
Crime Startles and Shocks the Entire Hills Country.
Well loved Priest Lured to His Death on a Plea that His Holy Duties were
Required by a dying man—
Shot down by His Assassin in Cold Blood

Father Belknap's casket was barely closed when rumors about the motive for the murder began to circulate. Was this the devious plot of the Ku Klux Klan? Vicious anti-Catholic rhetoric often turns into actual deeds.

The Ku Klux Klan, along with the Masons quickly spread the rumor that Father Belknap was involved in an illicit affair with a married blonde. They promulgated the fiction that the woman's husband killed the priest in a rage of passion. The lie stated that Father Belknap was caught in bed with the woman and shot. Then the priest's body was hauled away and dumped near Poorman Gulch.[14]

All the rumors vanished when the facts began to surface. Father Belknap's overcoat had bullet holes in it—unlikely one would engage in an illicit affair in one's overcoat. Footprints at the crime scene indicated that he was killed

Headline in the *Lead Daily Call* newspaper on Wednesday, October 26, 1921. *Courtesy of the* Lead Daily Call.

Father Belknap lying murdered on Poorman's Gulch Road in Lead, South Dakota. *Courtesy of the* Lead Daily Call.

where they found him. Clearly, the body was not hauled from somewhere else and dumped there.[15]

Charles Rambow, a local Ku Klux Klan researcher and presenter, said that the KKK most likely floated these rumors in hopes of smearing the reputation of the popular priest and the local Catholic diocese.

Oddly, these fictions would enable the KKK to take credit for the crime and build the Klan's reputation as a force of leadership in the community. However, the public outcry and denial of the trumped-up rumors forced the KKK to retreat for a time from the fabrications and stay in the shadows. The Knights of Columbus offered a $500 reward for information leading to the murderer's capture; the county followed suit.

The year 1921 was a bad one for Catholic priests, not only in South Dakota but in the nation as well. In Birmingham, Alabama, Father James Edwin Coyle was assigned to serve the Cathedral of St. Paul. The South was not a great environment to be Catholic at the time. "The promise of jobs had brought people flooding into cities like Birmingham. However they were regarded by the locals as foreigners and followers of an alien and dangerous creed. The Ku Klux Klan was entering a new phase of nativism activity."[16]

Nativism was a powerful tenet of the KKK in which members tried to keep America 100 percent American, safe from foreign influence, particularly Catholics and Jews.

Rumors abounded. There was a widespread belief that organizations like the Knights of Columbus were stockpiling weapons. On the order of the pope, Catholics would rise up and overthrow the government. "Some states passed laws allowing warrantless searches of convents and other religious buildings for these weapons. Anti-Catholic riots broke out in various southern states. In 1916, Birmingham elected people from nativist groups to local offices. Catholics were fired from state jobs. Businesses were harassed for employing Catholics. Guards needed to be added to churches. Some Catholic churches were burned."[17]

The tinderbox finally exploded in 1921. That year, Ruth Stephenson, the daughter of a Methodist minister and Klansman, Reverend Edwin R. Stephenson, converted to Catholicism against her father's wishes. Birmingham was not only a heavily segregated city but also a hotbed of anti-Catholic sentiment with a significance Ku Klux Klan presence.

On August 11, Father James Coyle, an Irish immigrant, presided at the wedding between Ruth Stephenson, aged eighteen and a "dark-skinned" Puerto Rican man named Pedro Gussman.

About an hour after the wedding, Father Coyle was relaxing in a rocking chair on his rectory porch. It was hot, and he was enjoying the shade. Suddenly, an enraged former barber and member of the Ku Klux Klan, Reverend Stephenson, walked up and fired three shots, killing Father Coyle. He died instantly.

Then the killer, Reverend Stephenson, turned himself in at the police station a block away.

Stephenson was charged with the priest's murder, and the case went to trial. The trial was a farce. The Ku Klux Klan raised funds for the defense. Stephenson hired four Klansman led by Hugo Black, future U.S. senator and Supreme Court justice, as his lawyer. The judge, William E. Fort, was a Klansman, as were the foreman and other members of the jury.

The trial started on October 17 with the peculiar plea of "not guilty and not guilty by reason of insanity." Reverend Stephenson was supposedly driven to insanity by his daughter Ruth's conversion and marriage to a Puerto Rican, they argued. The defense claimed Gussman was Black and leaned heavily into anti-Catholic sentiments. Stephenson was found not guilty by reason of insanity—and walked free. He never faced consequences from either the state or the Methodist Church. Stephenson returned to his position as "the marrying parson" at the local courthouse. He was given a seat of honor at Alabama Klan rallies.

No one was ever punished for the murder of Father Coyle.

After spending ten years as a U.S. senator, Hugo Black was appointed an associate justice of the U.S. Supreme Court by FDR, where he served until 1971.[18]

Father James Edwin Coyle, Catholic priest, murdered on August 11, 1921, in Birmingham, Alabama, with Ku Klux Klan approval and support. *www. encycopediaofalabama.org.*

Back in Lead, South Dakota law enforcement was stumped. Would the killer of Father Belknap ever be identified? Ever be tracked down? Ever caught? Yes? No? What part if any would the Ku Klux Klan have to do with this heinous death?

An article in the *Deadwood Pioneer-Times* of October 29, 1921, identified a major suspect: "Officials hot on the [trail] of Andrew Rolando, suspected slayer of Father Belknap."

The article recounted the murder: "Father A.B. Belknap, 30, of the St. Patrick's Cathedral in Lead, was found in Bender Park on the Poorman Gulch Road in south Lead in the early morning of Oct. 26. A medical examination of the body showed that he had been hit on the head and shot."

The article went on: "According to the testimony of various witnesses, law enforcement believed the murderer to be Andrew (Andrio) Rolando, 21, who came to Lead to work in the Homestake Mine."

The bizarre twists and turns of what happened next was researched and covered by journalist Kaija Swisher of the *Black Hills Pioneer* in three posts beginning on July 27, 2018.

From the *Deadwood Pioneer-Times* article:

> *Andrew Rolando quit his job at Homestake a few days before the murder....*
> *He met a certain Mary Krasovic of Butte, Montana who wanted to go*
> *home...and Rolando promised to take her in "his" car.*
>
> *They were to meet early Wednesday morning, but Rolando failed to*
> *show up....Krasovic said that she later met him, and he told her that his*
> *car had been stolen....Piecing together the testimony of witnesses, law*
> *enforcement officials believed at the time that the theft of Father Belknap's*
> *car was the motive, so Rolando could drive Krasovic to Butte. Belknap had*
> *complained that someone had tried to steal a car from the garage of the*
> *parsonage of Bishop J.J. Lawler a short time before.*
>
> *A .45 Colt revolver, an automobile hammer and a glove covered with*
> *blood were found in Rolando's room.*
>
> *Authorities learned that Rolando had arrived in Edgemont, S.D., after*
> *he had been kicked off a freight trail several times by railroad men because*
> *he had no money....A $2,000 reward was offered for Rolando's capture...*
> *but Rolando was nowhere to be found.*

Kaija's research continued from a March 18, 1932 edition of the *Deadwood-Times*:

> *Rolando thot* [sic] *to have killed Rev. Vraiden; Man answering his*
> *description is under surveillance....Belknap's family tried to connect*
> *Rolando to the disappearance of a priest in Illinois. Father John A.*
> *Vraniak, of Virden, Ill., who disappeared under circumstances that led*
> *authorities to believe he was murdered. Apparently, papers collected from*
> *Rolando's home indicated that he had visited Vraiden in the past...and*
> *Rolando was known to be strongly antagonistic, almost to a point where*
> *it was a mania with him against priests and anything connected with the*
> *Catholic church.*[19]

Then the case of Father Belknap's murder became really weird. News from the October 17, 1932 edition of the *Lead Daily Call* revealed:

> *A priest in Ontario, Canada, confessed to murdering Belknap. Theodore*
> *Paul Hucal of Sudbury, Ontario, confesses in October. Hucal claimed to*
> *have arrived in Lead in September 1921, that he borrowed a cap and coat*
> *from Rolando the night of October 26, that he lured Belknap from his*

residence, and that he shot Belknap at the top of Poorman Hill. Hucal further claims he paid Rolando $50 on one occasion, $500 on another, and $1400 on another to play the role of suspect in the murder and aided him to make a getaway.

According to local records, however, Hucal did not arrive in Lead until well after Belknap's murder.

Bishop Lawler…reconfirmed beliefs that Hucal could not have committed the crime due to the fact that he did not arrive in Lead until after the crime was committed.[20]

The October 26, 1949 edition of the *Deadwood Pioneer-Times*—on the twenty-eighth anniversary of Belknap's murder—related, "An extensive search for [Rolando] followed and led into Wyoming where the trail grew dim and finally faded out and with faced the hope of solving the crime."[21]

In the East River region, similar hate acts against Catholicism broke out, such as the one in Groton, South Dakota. In 1921, Groton's St. John's Catholic Church building suffered vandalism, ostensibly by Klansmen. They broke memorial windows, trampled vestments, battered the furnace with an axe and threw tomatoes around the sanctuary.

These assaults and others led to the founding of the Knights of the Flaming Circle—mostly Knights of Columbus members—who prepared for possible confrontation with the Klan.[22]

Parishioners of the St. Joseph's Catholic Church in Wessington, South Dakota, remember hearing the stories about how the Klan had once been in the area. Their priest, Father O'Neill, told some of his flock how he kept a firearm in the rectory because he feared that one day the Klan might attack him or the church. Most likely Father O'Neill had heard of the tragic murder of Father Belknap at Lead.

2

THE ANTI-CATHOLIC RANT

I t was fall haying time in 1892 when John Norberg and his brother
Peter came back for a visit to Dalesburg in Clay County, South Dakota.
They had attended school in Dalesburg and then left for Omaha. Now
they were back. They were fired up. Influenced by and as members of
the "APA," they came on a mission—full throttle!

The APA, the American Protective
Association, was an American anti-
Catholic secret society in Iowa. It was
founded by Henry F. Bowers with a few
friends on March 13, 1887. By 1896, the
APA claimed a six-figure membership
at its peak. As an attorney in Clinton,
Iowa, leading the APA, Bowers demanded
Catholics remove themselves from office
because he and the APA saw Catholics as
having dual loyalties. The APA claimed
that Catholics congregated in areas of
large cities, preventing the election of
non-Catholics, and that 60 to 90 percent
of government employees were Catholic.
The APA's ideology espoused the beliefs
that Catholics threatened the public school
systems, that the army and navy were

Henry F. Bowers from Clinton, Iowa,
founder of the anti-Catholic American
Protective Association. *Illustration from
the* Logansport [IN] Pharos-Tribune,
May 22, 1896, 22. Wikicommons.

almost entirely "Romanized," that priests desecrated the flag, that the federal government was controlled by Jesuits and that Roman Catholics were under complete political control of the pope. The APA claimed that Catholics were required to obey the church's laws when they were in conflict with those of the state, citing the papal encyclical issued by Leo XIII on January 10, 1890, *Sapientiae Christianae*.[23]

Brothers John and Peter Norberg, sons of Swedish immigrant Christine Norberg, galloped into Clay County, South Dakota, "hair on fire," pontificating and selling APA ideology.

They instilled into the Dalesburg and Clay County citizens a bone-chilling fear that the Catholics from adjacent Union County were planning an uprising against the Protestants.

The Norberg brothers preached that every Catholic church provided an armory for the storage of arms and ammunition. The Norbergs claimed and warned that when the signal was given, the Catholics would rise up and kill their Protestant neighbors wherever found.

August Peterson, who emigrated from Norway to Clay County in 1888, was fascinated by the stories of his fellow Clay County immigrants. He collected those stories and others and published them in a historical document titled "The Swedes Who Settled in Clay County, South Dakota."

A great-grandson of August Peterson, Rick Lingberg, in a 2015 post said, "You may never [have] heard of the plan of Union County Catholics to siege the Clay County Protestants, but in 1892 many of the Scandinavians were sure more than rosary beads were coming over the wall."[24]

A meeting was called at the Dalesburg school house to discuss the situation and the house was fairly well filled in the evening. The writer (August Peterson) was present. One of those who was particularly excited about the situation was Andrew J. Cole, who testified he had seen a black, enclosed wagon, hauling ammunition from Garryowen to Beresford and back, with a cross marked behind. The people were thoroughly aroused, and a committee was elected to make a definite and further investigation, and to provide ways and means to having everyone protect themselves and their families. Members of the committee included Peter Heglin and Oscar Sundstrom, and possibly John Norin, if not mistaken.

The consensus of opinion was, among those who attended the meeting referred to, that everybody who believed there was danger, buy themselves a rifle and to have it loaded in their houses, ready for the momentous day when the Catholics came. The hardware merchants in the adjoining towns made a thriving business in selling every shooting iron they had in stock, and many homes in the community were armed for the coming eventful day.

As a matter of fact, nothing happened, and the people finally cooled down on the idea, until at last those who had taken the most prominent stand in the excitement, felt rather cheap and ashamed when the matter was discussed. The A.P.A. organization flourished for a season, just like the Ku Klux Klan in later years, and thus another hallucination died a natural death.[25]

Correspondents affiliated with the APA informed the governor of Nebraska and a U.S. senator from Minnesota that arms were being shipped to priests in Michigan and Nebraska in coffins or in boxes labeled "holy wine."[26]

The American Protective Association thrived, with numbers estimated in South Dakota at three thousand members, until 1896. But the organization's collapse was rapid. Only a hollow shell remained by 1898. The hatred-spewing organization totally died when founder Henry Bowers passed in 1911.

The anti-Catholic seeds planted by the APA lay dormant until 1915. Then, like thistles, a reborn Ku Klux Klan revived, grew and harvested latent seeds of hatred.

Anti-Catholic tenets, rhetoric and actions flourished into the 1920s. Father O'Neill of St. Joseph's Catholic Church in Wessington, South Dakota, once told wary parishioners that he kept a firearm in the rectory because he feared that one day the Klan might attack him or the church.

Tales of the "Catholic menace" flourished. Klan frenzy legitimized preposterous stories such as this one during the national presidential election. They deeply believed that the Roman pope planned to seize the government. If Al Smith, a Catholic, was elected president, the pope would have a secret underground tunnel dug to the basement of the White House so that the pope could hightail it over and order the president what to do. It boggles a rational person's mind how the pope in the Vatican in Rome could accomplish such a feat. Fantasy? Miracle? Delusion?

Although the era in which South Dakota became a state is known for its anti-Catholicism, the phenomenon dates back to the Reformation of the sixteenth century in Europe. When Protestants began to break away from the united Christian church headquartered in Rome, they published derisive critiques and quasi-historical propaganda regarding Roman Catholicism.

The ensuing religious wars between Protestants and Catholics in Europe, always tied to national loyalties, only deepened sectarian divide.[27]

Anti-Catholicism arrived in the "new world" the day the Puritans stepped on American soil in Massachusetts. Appearing with their felt hats, breeches, garters, bonnets, aprons and flintlock arms, the Puritans left the "old world" and brought Puritanism as a new way of life.

Puritanism was a religious reform movement in the late sixteenth and seventeenth centuries that sought to purify the Church of England of remnants of the Roman Catholic popery. Calvinist theology and polity proved to be major influences in the formation and practice of Puritan teachings. With an emphasis on a covenant relationship with God, preaching and moral living, Puritans rejected much of that which was characteristic of Anglican ritual. They viewed Anglican ritual and life as "popish idolatry."

Eventually, the Puritans of New England evolved into the Congregational Church. According to Ray Allen Billington, in his *Protestant Crusade*, the Congregationalists of New England became known for their long-standing "hatred of Popery."

Anti-Catholicism in America emerged due to the mass immigration of Catholics in the mid-nineteenth century and the fear that Catholics could and would change the American nation. Historian Jay Dolan blames much of the discrimination against Catholics in this period on immigration.[28]

Of the many European ethnic groups, none demonstrated a stronger degree of solidarity in the United States than Irish Catholics. Irish Catholics emphasized economic solidarity, collective action and politics as keys to improve their economic status while resisting gross discrimination.

From the early nineteenth century into the 1920s, Irish Catholics were confronted with waves of anti-Catholic sentiment. The evangelical revivals of the nineteenth century spawned a "No Popery" movement. A popular children's game was Break the Pope's Neck.

Break the Pope's Neck was first written about on December 18, 1773, in a journal by Philip Vickers Fithian, a tutor living on a Virginia plantation. The game involved spinning a plate and letting it fall.

The 1920s witnessed a renewed outburst of anti-Catholic sentiment. Legislatures in the South, Midwest and West, influenced by the staunchly anti-Catholic Ku Klux Klan, tried to require daily Bible readings from the Protestant version of the Bible.

In Ole Rolvaag's novel *Peder Victorious*, the character Beret fights to preserve her family's Norwegian heritage on the Dakota prairie and castigates her son Peder for fraternizing with Irish Catholics, "those people" of a "dangerous" faith. Another Norwegian settler in *Peder Victorious* insists that "before he'd let any of his marry a Catholic he'd see him buried alive!" The prospect of such a wedding causes a "terrible rumpus" and "awful commotion" in the settlement. Beret denounces the "wickedness of Peder's consorting with an Irish Catholic girl," telling him, "If the day should come that you get yourself mixed up with the Irish, then you have lost your mother—that I could not live through!"

She then declares with conviction, "You can't mix wheat and potatoes in the same bin."[29]

My college history professor, Lynwood Oyos, wrote in "Lutherans Discover Each Other and American Values" that "Norwegian-Lutheran families were particularly tight-knit and found it 'very upsetting' if a family member 'associated too closely with someone of another denomination or nationality.'"

When I was growing up in Day County, South Dakota, it was a serious breach of social norms for "mixed" marriages to take place. My Norwegian/German parents, devout Lutherans, looked askance at Lutheran/Catholic marriages. The Catholic rule demanding that the Protestant partner convert to Catholicism or raise the children in the Catholic faith was seen as unfair and rigid.

"Fish eaters" was a derogatory term we used flippantly and insensitively toward our Catholic neighbors, referring to their fasting practice of not eating meat on Fridays. *Awful Disclosures of Maria Monk* was a typical anti-Catholic popular book circulating and poisoning readers.

During the national surge in Ku Klux Klan activity in the 1920s, it was the anti-Catholic aspect of the Klan that prompted many of the approximately three thousand South Dakotans to join. In fact, when the KKK planned meetings in South Dakota in the 1920s, it emphasized that only Protestants could attend.[30]

In eastern South Dakota, the Catholic Church also became a focal point for Klansmen, who targeted Catholic "card parties, dances and booze parties." The Klan newspaper specifically mentioned card parties "put on in the Catholic churches in Madison, Nunda, and Ramona," calling them "fronts for dances and liquor parties with the sole intent of gaining converts to Catholicism."

"Catholics in the Black Hills towns of Lead and Sturgis were subjected to cross burnings and dynamite blasts. One interviewee recalled the school superintendent in Rapid City being terminated for refusing to fire all Catholic schoolteachers at the behest of the KKK."[31]

The issue of Prohibition provided divisiveness and friction between the Catholics and Protestants. The Ku Klux Klan pounced on this issue. They listed bootlegging, among the demons of society, and they took it on full bore to eliminate it. When Episcopal bishop William Hobart Hare supported an exemption for sacramental alcohol, there was an outcry from the Methodists, the State Prohibition League and the WCTU (Woman's Christian Temperance Union). I remember my mother, Nora, was a member of the WCTU and supported the temperance movement in South Dakota.

The school issue was a meat cleaver between Catholics and Protestants. The Ku Klux Klan, claiming its Protestant bent, charged that the pope was using parochial schools to infiltrate, brainwash and train Catholics to take over America. The Klan hypocritically defended separation of church and state while promoting Protestant religious content in public schools. (One source, Jon Lauck in his "You Can't Mix Wheat and Potatoes in the Same Bin: Anti-Catholicism in Early Dakota," describes and expands on this conflicting contrast.)

The burst of anti-Catholicism nationally and the intense criticism of sectarian education corresponded to the years when the Catholic population in Dakota territory grew most rapidly. The church pressured its priests and parishioners to build school systems for Catholic children.

In 1879, when Martin Marty became prefect apostolic of Dakota Territory, one year prior to being named bishop, there were twenty Catholic churches and twelve priests in Dakota. By 1884, with the Great Dakota Boom in full swing, Marty reported overseeing eighty-two churches and forty-five priests.[32] One 1885 publication noted the existence of "many parochial schools of the Church."[33]

When Marty left South Dakota in 1894, the state had 143 Catholic churches, sixty-eight priests and many Catholic schools; six Catholic hospitals and numerous Catholic high schools were founded, and Benedictine, Mercy, Saint Joseph, Saint Vincent DePaul, Presentation and Saint Francis sisters established orders in the state. By 1906, 177 Catholic churches and eighty-two priests served seventy-nine thousand Catholics in South Dakota. By the early twentieth century, there were eight Catholic high schools and forty-four elementary schools in the state.[34]

In contrast to the Catholic schools, the public or common schools bore a strong Protestant imprint. The New England Puritan model helped shape South Dakota public education. One of the leaders of the common school movement in South Dakota was William H.H. Beadle. The honor of his name would one day be attached to General Beadle College at Madison, South Dakota. Beadle was a Mason, a Republican and a Union veteran of the Civil War. He maintained a close relationship with Reverend Joseph Ward, pastor of the influential Congregational Church in Yankton. The Congregational Church continued the influence of New England Puritanism in Dakota.

The Ku Klux Klan adopted the content and style of this flavor of Protestantism in their fiery opposition to Roman Catholics.

3

WHITE SHEETS AND HOODS

A BRIEF HISTORY

It was December 23, 1865, when six defeated young Confederate veteran officers met in the small, poverty-stricken town of Pulaski, Tennessee. The Civil War had just ended the previous May 9, 1865. The six veterans gathered around a stove in a law office inside a brick building. Gloom hung over them as a black cloud. They were penniless, had no plans or purpose for the future.

Christmas joy and celebrations in two days seemed a distant dream. They felt it. They knew it.

They needed to jar themselves out of their depression.

"Boys," one of them said, "let's start something to break the monotony and cheer up our mothers and girls. Let's start a social club of some kind."[35]

They agreed to meet soon again to plan. They met at the home of Colonel Thomas Martin, a prominent citizen of Pulaski. What would they name their fledgling social club?

Recalling their college Greek, they chose the word for band or circle—*KuKlos*. "Ku Klux," a barbarization of *Kuklos*, was suggested by one of the boys and at once adopted. Since the six were mostly of Scots Irish descent, they added another Gaelic word—*Klan*. Their imaginations stirred, using alliteration, they came up with an inglorious name: Ku Klux Klan.

Ku Klux Klan stuck. It would become the name of an organization subverting and confounding American history to the present day.

The six colluded to have fun. They wanted to lift the spirits of their neighbors. They started by robing themselves in wild and outlandish costumes. They draped themselves in white sheets and pillowcases. Their horses, too, were draped in white as the six merrymakers rode down and about the countryside, bemusing their neighbors. The pranks, however, seemingly harmless, morphed into an unexpected result.

The southern Confederate states lay defeated and crushed. With the surrender of General Robert E. Lee and his twenty-eight thousand troops at Appomattox on April 9, 1965, to General Ulysses S. Grant, the battle was over. Citizens of the South had suffered greatly from the effects of the war. Many lost their homes, and plantations, as well as friends and loved ones to the war. The South, now pale, anemic and emaciated, struggled to find its soul. The war had ended, technically. But peace and tranquility? Guerrilla warfare, outlawry and opportunism sprouted like weeds. Was help on the way?

During Reconstruction, from 1865 to 1877, two unwelcome hornets appeared on the scene with mixed intentions: the scalawags and the carpetbaggers. Scalawag was a pejorative term for a white southerner who supported the federal plan of Reconstruction. A scalawag was one who joined with Black freedmen and the carpetbaggers in support of Republican Party policies.

A carpetbagger earned the derogatory term as an individual who came from the North carrying nothing more than a satchel (carpetbag) with intentions to prey on the misfortunes of the South. Some carpetbaggers arrived with good intentions, many others for personal greed and political gain.

Unscrupulous southerners (scalawags) joined with northern carpetbaggers to form a radical coalition in order to control most branches of government.

They recruited freed African Americans. This coalition then armed their African American recruits into militia bands that paraded publicly— rifles on their shoulders. This new show of strength frightened many white southerners. The southerners became increasingly wary of the increasing power and presence of Black people.

Amid this fear and uncertainty, the Pulaski pranksters began their first rides. Quickly they realized riding their ghost-like horses and white-garbed appearances were having an unexpected effect.

People saw apparitions. Ghosts appearing. Suddenly, out of the night the Klansmen rode to carpetbaggers' political rallies and broke them up. Haunted pranks turned political.

A ghostly rider would appear before the hut of a black follower of the Carpetbaggers. The visitor would stop his horse and ask for a drink of water. Prepared before hand, he would conceal a leather bag hidden under his robe and as the black man stared in disbelief he would drink three bucketfuls of water remarking that he had traveled a thousand miles in the last 24 hours. He would then add, "that's best water I have had since I was killed at the Battle of Shiloh."

As a final grisly touch he might stretch out a hand from beneath the white robe and show his black host a human skull. Of course the frightened observer quickly fled.[36]

Sometimes the ghostly riders carried skeletal hands concealed in their sleeves and insisted on shaking hands with the Black man. These "childish" pranks had an amazing effect on many southerners who were still chained by fear and superstition.

More and more wild tales abounded in those early years. Imaginations soared. White figures on white-clad horses were reported sailing in the skies.

Barraged by contrived imaginations and propaganda, the populace and especially Black southerners shook in their boots.

In three months, the Pulaski Klan grew. It burst out of its original little law office building and purchased a new meeting place on the edge of town. From that modest gathering site, the blight and curse of a campaign of fear and intimidation metastasized.

The KKK continued to ride the countryside disrupting carpetbaggers' political rallies. People fled the rallies out of fear. Word quickly spread across the South about sightings of masked and hooded marauders everywhere. Fighting the carpetbaggers and keeping the Black population controlled appealed to many potential KKK members.

The Klan grew rapidly. A leader was needed to guide and control the growing group. Separate Klaverns, as the newly formed local groups were called, could not be allowed to spring up all over the South and go their own way without direction.

A delegation traveled to Virginia to appeal to General Robert E. Lee to lead the movement. Being in poor health, he declined. He wrote a letter saying he approved of the Klan, although his backing must be "invisible." When the letter was read later, the word *invisible* struck a chord, and the label the "Invisible Empire" has lasted to the present day.

In May 1866, General Nathan Bedford Forrest, who was one of the most successful and celebrated Civil War leaders from the South, happened to hear about the Klan movement started in Pulaski. Intrigued, he saw the group as something to rein in the injustices being inflicted on the South by the scalawag-carpetbagger regimes.

Forrest hurried to Nashville to connect with Captain John Morton, who had been chief of his artillery.

"'John,' Forrest said, 'I hear this Ku Klux Klan is organized in Nashville, and I know you are in it.' Morton drove Forrest out to a lonely spot in dense woods. Morton stopped the buggy in which they were riding, turned to Forrest and said, 'General, do you say you want to join the Ku Klux Klan?' 'Hold up your right hand,' Morton told him. Forrest raised his hand and his former aide administered the preliminary oath of the order. As he finished taking the oath, Forrest said, 'John, that's the worst swearing I ever did.'"[37]

At a later meeting, Nathan Bedford Forrest was elected the KKK commander, with the title "Grand Wizard of the Invisible Empire." He immediately employed military discipline and order. He established absolute power over the Klan members. Many of the men were former Confederate soldiers who trusted him completely. The KKK gave members a sense of belonging and purpose. The Klan established the code of secrecy, which offered safety from non-Klan members.

Under Forrest, the Klan operated in defiance of northern soldiers sent south to keep the South in subjugation. In 1868, the Klan continued to exert its power. It vowed to rid the South of carpetbaggers, Blacks and anyone who supported any opposition. It stole the opposition's goods and beat, tortured and hanged them in the nearest tree. The murders or lynching took place in the center of town where they were hanged in front of all to see. This intimidation was profoundly effective. It struck fear into anyone who would have anything to do with carpetbaggers or Blacks.

Forrest advertised Klan power dramatically when he engineered one of the first grand parades in Pulaski on July 4, 1867. In deathlike stillness, Ku Klux Klan marchers entered the city from four different roads. Not a word was spoken. They marched and counter marched throughout the town for two

Nathan Beford Forrest, general in the Confederate army and the first Grand Wizard of the Ku Klux Klan from 1867 to 1869. *Library of Congress.*

hours. Then they disappeared, confounding the observers. townsfolks and rural visitors alike were totally mystified.

A secret war burned between the scalawag-carpetbagger forces and white-robed Klansmen during the Reconstruction era. Carpetbaggers' growing rule backed by their own militia and voting power of recently freed Black men fanned the fires of white disgust and hatred.

HISTORICAL KKK OVERVIEW

Three powerful KKK social movements wormed their ways in and through the tissues and membranes of U.S. history.

The first Klan (1865–1877), founded at Pulaski, Tennessee, in 1865, masqueraded as a clownish prank-inspired social club. It celebrated secret rituals, costumes featuring white robes, masks, pointy hats and spooky night rides. This nascent club spread quickly throughout the South. Klan members promised to defend the Constitution and help widows, orphans and the oppressed.

However, when Black citizens were given freedom, civil rights and the power to vote, the Klan resorted to intimidation, violence and the rope (lynching). Carpetbaggers and scalawags pounced into the political vacuum of the defeated South, igniting battles with the KKK.

Led by General Nathan Bedford Forrest, the first KKK movement gradually declined and expired with a quiet gasp in 1877 when Reconstruction ended. The Klan disbanded when it became clear that Jim Crow laws would secure white supremacy across the country. (On July 9, 2020, Tennessee's State Capitol Commission voted to remove the bust of Nathan Bedford Forrest from the state capitol. The actual removal took place on July 23, 2021, whereby the bust was promptly placed in the Tennessee's State Capitol Museum.)

The second Klan (1915–1930) movement snaked its way into American society beginning in 1915 and ending around 1930. Its founder, bombastic ex-preacher William Joseph Simmons, at a clandestine meeting on top of Stone Mountain, Georgia, concocted and organized a dubious fraternal charitable organization. Voilà—the Ku Klux Klan reborn. After 1919, the newly revived Klan grew rapidly. By the mid 1920s, it had organized in every state. This revived Klan astutely exploited the fears and anxieties of post–World War I America. "The Klan's promise to preserve traditional values and morals gave people a sense of power, fraternity and security."[38]

The Klan's primary message boasted that it stood for law and order, traditional morality and especially 100 percent Americanism. Cleverly, the Klan tailored its message to meet local issues and concerns. Targets, besides Black people, were Jews, radicals, immigrants, Mexicans, Asians (such as the Chinese population in Lead/Deadwood) and Catholics.

The Klan had few qualms about using pressure and even violence to achieve its goals. In the South, the Klan perpetuated public whippings, tar and featherings, lynchings and brutal homicides. In Texas and Oklahoma, there were as many as one thousand victims of Klan violence.

By the end of 1944, the U.S. government had sued the Klan for back taxes. It collapsed and disbanded.

The third Klan (1946/1950–present) movement arose to oppose civil rights in the 1950s and 1960s. It involved numerous bombings and murders in the South. One of the most egregious acts was the killing of four young girls attending Sunday school at the 16th Street Baptist Church in Birmingham, Alabama, in 1963. The murders of civil rights workers Andrew Goodman, James Chaney and Michael Schwerner in Mississippi gained the attention of the nation and the White House. White supremacy, the Klan's despicable core value, continued into the 1970s. Julian Bond, social activist, leader of the civil rights movement and co-founder of SNCC (Student Nonviolent Coordinating Committee), asserted, "Then white supremacy went on into the 2016s" and to the present.

4

RISING FROM THE ASHES

A REVIVAL OF THE KLAN

From 1877 to 1890, a populist movement attempted to form an alliance between Blacks and whites.

The Klan no longer terrorized the cities and countryside. Violence and lynching were perpetuated most often by lawless rednecks against poor whites and Blacks as well. Yet hatred simmered below the surface. It manifested itself in continued segregation and demeaning of the Black citizenry; though freed by the Civil War, they were humiliated to a life hardly better than slavery. Jim Crow laws infected much of southern society. This simmering racial hatred was largely confined to the South—until 1915.

About two weeks before the showing of the movie *The Birth of a Nation* in Atlanta, Georgia, sixteen ghostly figures, barely discerned in the overcast night, climbed the granite crest of Stone Mountain. Stone Mountain is a quartz monzonite dome sixteen miles east of Atlanta. At its summit, the elevation is 1,686 feet above sea level. The gradual climb of 825 feet above the surrounding area provides a modest challenge for hikers. Two elderly Klansman—their accompaniment representing the Ku Klux Klan of past decades—joined the sixteen.

When the men finished the rocky trail to the summit, they paused for a rest. No one talked. Only whispers. Then a strange and mysterious confab began. The organizer, Colonel William Joseph Simmons, led the gathering. He unfurled an American flag, then erected a crude cross. Beside the Bible, a sword lay on the makeshift stone altar. The altar propped up the sixteen-foot cross. The upright post and its transverse bar, soaked in a mixture of gasoline

Colonel William J. Simmons, Protestant preacher and fraternal organizer who founded and led the Second Movement of the Ku Klux Klan from 1915 to 1922. *National Photo Company Collection, Library of Congress.*

and kerosene, were ready. Simmons then explained the significance of the sword. It had been used in wounding a Confederate soldier and had killed two Yankees in the Civil War. Next a solemn Klan oath was administered by Nathan Bedford Forrest's grandson Nathan Bedford Forrest III. In unison, the gathered novices pledged allegiance to the Invisible Empire, Knights of the Ku Klux Klan. Simmons struck a flame. The cross burst into a fiery plume.

The second movement of the Klan was reborn.

With Simmons's blueprint for a revived Klan organization in place, plus the power of the showstopper movie *The Birth of a Nation*, a cultural tsunami began to roll in.

Colonel William Joseph Simmons, an itinerant Methodist preacher, honed his oratorical skills for twelve years by preaching in poor churches in the backwoods of Alabama and Florida. As an effective speaker, he had an unusual affinity for alliteration. Simmons preached on "Women Weddings and Wives," "Red Heads, Dead Heads and No Heads" and the "Kinship of Kourtship and Kissing."

However, he was eventually dismissed by his superiors for inefficiency and moral impairment.

He turned to sales and lodge work. He joined multiple groups, such as the Masons, Knights Templar, Woodmen of the World and other fraternal organizations. He was conferred the title "Colonel" for his success in commanding five regiments of the Woodmen.

Through what Simmons describes as a spiritual experience coupled with his passion and vow that a great patriotic fraternal organization be established, he dreamed of a memorial to the heroes of our nation.

When he was injured in a car accident and ended up in rehab for three months, he drafted plans for a new fraternal organization. His concept was authoritarian. He would be the Imperial Wizard of the Invisible Empire. All power he would dictate. There would be eight districts, each headed by a Grand Dragon. Grand Titans would lead provinces. Exalted Cyclopes would command the local Klaverns. Fundraisers would be known as Kleagles.

Simmons then wrote a fifty-four-page guidebook called the Kloran. It contained secret mumbo jumbo jargon, rites and joining rituals.

Typically, after a newly recruited candidate agreed to join the Klan, a joining ritual was performed. The novitiate would be anointed oil from the sacred altar with these words,

With this transparent, life giving, powerful God-given fluid, more precious and far more significant than all sacred oils of the ancients, I set you apart from the men of your daily association to the great and honorable task you have voluntarily allotted yourselves as citizen of the Invisible Empire.

Sometime after the Stone Mountain vows were exchanged, Simmons gathered ninety recruits for the new Klan. "Each member paid him a ten dollar initiation fee. And to each he sold the white garb of the order and life insurance."[39]

For the first five years, the Klan grew slowly in Alabama, Georgia and across the South. When America entered World War I in 1917, the Klan began to gain more strength. Already aligned to patriotism, the Klan grew into its element. America had to be protected from the "evil" Germans, Catholics, Jews, Socialists, Blacks and union leaders.

In 1918, the great Klan tide began to swell. Patriotic parades flourished everywhere. In thousands of parades, the white-clothed, pointy-hatted Klan marched, holding high the American flag. When World War I ended,

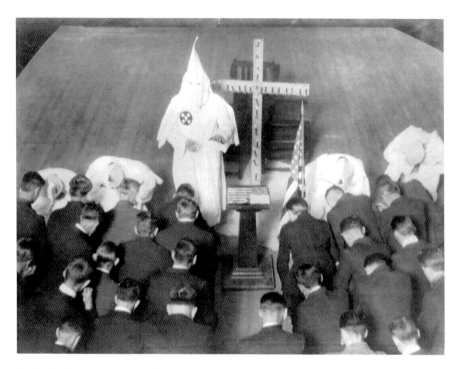

Typical initiation rite for receiving new members into the Klavern. *Library of Congress.*

fear and uncertainty descended on the nation. The communists took over Russia. A depression loomed. The times were ripe for hysteria. What a time for the Klan's clarion call to 100 percent Americanism.

Simmons, a spellbinding orator, though an impractical dreamer, had little organizing ability. The Ku Klux Klan needed skilled leadership quickly. It required fast-tracked public relations—a propaganda blitz by someone. That someone appeared in the team of Edward Young Clarke and Elizabeth Tyler. The duo signed a contract with Simmons and put their Southern Publicity Association company to work. They began by getting 80 percent of every ten-dollar membership fee they collected. They also required two dollars out of the membership fees that the Klan collected. The team played up the angst of the times. They identified the menace to America as the work of foreigners, radicals, Catholics, Jews and Blacks. They strong-armed the public, insisting that only 100 percent Americans and white Protestants could join the Klan.

A typical Klavern meeting dedicating (similar to Baptism) a hooded baby. Triangle Studio of Photography, 1924. *Library of Congress.*

Colonel Simmons emphasized the Klans' new pitch in dramatic fashion.... Towering above an audience of Georgia Klansmen, he said not a word as he drew a Colt automatic from one pocket and plunked it down on the table before him. Still silent, he took a revolver from another pocket and thumped that down on the table too. Then in one final, dramatic gesture, he whipped out a bowie knife and plunged it, the blade quivering, into the middle of his arsenal on the table. "Now," he thundered, "let the niggers, Catholics, Jews and all others who disdain my imperial wizardry come on." The campaign of racial and religious hatred had begun.[40]

From June 1920, when the Clarke/Tyler team signed the contract, to October 1921, the Klan grew to over 100,000 members.[41]

During this time, the Klan soared into the highest heavens and sank into the lowest gutter. Members preached piously the principles of the old-time Protestant religion—and at the same time under the cloak of holiness and godliness they practiced whippings, lynchings and murders.

Many Protestant ministers were duped into sympathy for the Klan. Nationally, it is estimated forty thousand ministers were recruited to preach the gospel of the Klan. Their messages poured forth from pulpits and lecture halls—100 percent Americanism, motherhood, chastity, temperance, the flag, the Bible and morality. With word and sword, they vowed to fight all enemies of the Klan. The enemy? A pamphlet described it this way:

> *Every criminal, every gambler, every thug, every libertine, every girl ruiner, every home wrecker, every wife beater, every dope peddler, every moonshiner, every crooked politician, every pagan Papist priest, every shyster lawyer, every K. of C., every white slaver, every brothel madam, every Rome controlled newspaper, every black spider—is fighting the Klan. Think it over. Which side are you on?*

The Clarke/Tyler recruitment campaign went exceedingly well for fifteen months. Hustlers (Kleagles) scooping up the 100,000-plus members raked in, at $10 per head, up to over $1 million. The Clarke/Tyler team's success seemed unstoppable.

Then the *New York World* newspaper began a twenty-one-day exposé of corruption and immorality in the Klan. This disclosure by the *World* brought to light the hypocrisy of the Klan, which ostentatiously proclaimed the protection of pure white womanhood. Clarke and Tyler had been arrested, less than fully clothed and less than sober, during a police raid on a brothel. The scandal rocked the Klan—for a time.

Though set back temporarily by shady scandals, the Ku Klux Klan nonetheless continued to spread.

American life still seemed to be threatened on every side. Dire perceptions invited solutions. The Klan was the solution.

Then the Ku Klux Klan leadership changed. Hiram Wesley Evans joined a clandestine gaggle of activists including Tyler, Clarke and D.C. Stephenson in a "coup" against William Joseph Simmons.

Simmons fell victim to a demotion to a lower "emperor" status. Eventually, he was expelled completely.

Evans gained power at the November 22, 1922 Klonvokation in Atlanta, Georgia. Dr. Evans, an Ashland, Alabama dentist, proudly usurped and wore the crown: imperial wizard of the Knights of the Ku Klux Klan.

His credentials belied his actions. As a member of the Disciples of Christ Church, Free Masons, Shriners and the KKK, he had led a group that kidnapped and tortured a Black bellhop, accusing the man of being

Imperial Wizard Hiram Wesley Evans leading a Ku Klu Klan parade, marching down Pennsylvania Avenue in Washington, D.C. *National Photo Company Collection, Library of Congress.*

involved with prostitutes in Dallas. He supported violence against minorities but discouraged vigilantism.

He promoted nativism, Protestant nationalism and white supremacy while condemning Catholicism, trade unions and communism. Evans said Jews were materialistic and resistant to assimilation. He claimed he was not antisemitic.

The Klan membership and influence rose in South Dakota. It grew in the entire Midwest. The highest numbers of the Ku Klux Klan swarmed in Indiana. Evans spoke to the largest Klan gathering in history on July

4, 1923, in rural Indiana. Over 200,000 gathered to listen and participate. Eventually, Evans marched with 30,000 Klansmen down Pennsylvania Avenue in Washington, D.C.

The Klan soon reached an astounding estimated membership of two and a half to six million in the United States. But acrimony reared its predicable ugly head. In January 1921, Evans and a group of Grand Dragons expelled the publicist Clarke. Clarke, who was critical of Evans's efforts to involve the Klan in politics. An ambitious upstart, David Curtis Stephenson, took over leadership in a failing KKK presence in Indiana. With an eye on power and eventually the White House, Stephenson developed the strongest KKK presence in the nation in Indiana. Now as Grand Dragon he became the new "Messiah." Then a breach split Imperial Wizard Evans and Grand Dragon Stephenson. They snarled and snipped. Lawsuits flew to and fro.

David Curtis "Steve" Stephenson, appointed Grand Dragon of the Indiana Ku Klux Klan, who rose to political prominence with ambitions for the White House. *Public domain.*

Stephenson liked women and whiskey. His downfall was twenty-eight-year-old Madge Oberholtzer. She was young and attractive, and he pursued her. Eventually, Stephenson assaulted her and was arrested. He was convicted of her abduction, forced intoxication and rape. His abuse led to her suicide attempt and eventual death. He was convicted for her death and sent to prison for life. He was released in 1956, thirty-one years later. Hardly anyone knew him as he walked out of jail. Mount Rushmore sculptor Gutzon Borglum befriended Stephenson, supported him and corresponded with him while in prison until Borglum's death on March 6, 1941.

5

THE ROLE AND POWER
OF THE MEDIA

In 1915, David Wark Griffith's movie *The Birth of a Nation* hit the silver screen. Its impact let loose a seismic cultural wave. In fact, *Birth of a Nation* bedazzled and handcuffed the minds and emotions of the entire nation—South Dakota included. It was explosive, mesmerizing, captivating.

One of the early showings of *The Birth of a Nation* was in North Dakota. "It appeared in Grand Forks, North Dakota in December 1915 and ran for a week to a packed house."[42]

The Birth of a Nation ran in the Black Hills area in early 1916, billed as "D.W. Griffith's masterpiece. It is a Story of Romance. It is a Story of Adventure. It is full of Human Interest and Emotion. Go to *The Birth of a Nation*."[43]

Many did. They walked away enthralled. Some quickly became sympathetic toward a fanciful view of the Ku Klux Klan.

The Birth of a Nation was based on an adaption of a novel and play written in 1905, *The Clansman: A Historical Romance of the Ku Klux Klan*, by Thomas Dixon Jr. The book was a melodramatic and vivid portrayal of the worst of Reconstruction.

It portrays Black people as unprincipled and wild. The book's love story centers on two beautiful southern girls, the image of saintly and pure womanhood. One of the girls is attacked by a Black man, throws herself over a nearby cliff and dies by suicide to save her virtue. The second girl, who is the heroine of the novel, is besieged in an isolated cabin. The Ku Klux Klan rides in and saves her.

Thomas Dixon's novel is set against Harriet Beecher Stowe's *Uncle Tom's Cabin*. Dixon presumptuously described his novel *The Birth of a Nation* as a sequel to Harriet Beecher Stowe's *Uncle Tom's Cabin*. The literary and content differences between the two are stark. The character of Gus in *The Clansman*, who is described as a horrible former slave and goes so far as to rape a woman, is the opposite of the kindly, benevolent Uncle Tom whom Harriet portrays as angelic.

Both books stirred up furious but opposite reactions. Harriet Beecher Stowe's *Uncle Tom's Cabin* was despised and banned throughout the South. *The Clansman* was ranted against in northern papers and society. Dixon revived the image of the flaming cross, which became the terrorizing symbol of the Ku Klux Klan in its second wave. Dixon was inspired by the historical practices of Scottish clans. This image also appears in Walter Scott's poem *Lady of the Lake* (1810).

Thomas Frederick Dixon Jr., author of eighteen novels, wrote *The Clansman: A Historical Romance of the Ku Klux Klan*, romanticizing southern white supremacy. Dixon's novel served as the basis for the script for *The Birth of a Nation*. The movie inspired the rebirth of the Second Movement of the Ku Klux Klan in the early twentieth century. *From* The Book Buyer.

Thomas Dixon Jr., a southern minister, dramatic preacher and lecturer, eventually wrote twenty-two novels. At Johns Hopkins University, he excelled as a brilliant and social student, befriending Woodrow Wilson.

Thomas Dixon grew up after the Civil War, during the Reconstruction period in South Carolina. He witnessed the government confiscation of farmland, coupled with the corruption of local politicians, the vengeful acts of the Union troops and general lawlessness. His father and maternal uncle Colonel Leroy McAfee, Grand Titan of the Invisible Empire, joined the Ku Klux Klan in order to bring order to the tumultuous times. Dixon remembered watching (first Klan movement) a parade of the Ku Klux Klan through the village streets on a moonlit night in 1869 when he was five years old. He recalled the account of the widow of a Confederate soldier who had served under uncle Colonel McAfee. The widow accused a Black man of the rape of her daughter. She sought the Dixon family for help. Dixon's mother praised the Klan after it had shot and hanged the alleged rapist in the town square.

As a lawyer, minister, actor, playwright and popular lecturer, Dixon did not join the Klan. He did, however, glorify and romanticize the movement. The dubious mission of controlling the Black population was made evident in his novels.

In his first trilogy, *The Leopard's Spots*, Dixon depicts how the Klan deals with a Black man who had asked a white woman to kiss him.

> *When the sun rose next morning the lifeless body of Tim Shelby was dangling from a rope tied to the iron rail of the balcony of the court house. His neck was broken and his body was hanging low—scarcely three feet from the ground. His thick lips had been split with a sharp knife and from his teeth hung this placard: "The answer of the Anglo-Saxon race to Negro lips that dare pollute with words the womanhood of the South. K.K.K."*[44]

Dixon's second novel, *The Clansman: A Historical Romance of the Ku Klux Klan*, served as the basis of a controversial play, which in turned caught the attention of movie maker David Wark Griffith.

Thomas Dixon's novel did not directly cause the resurrection of the new Ku Klux Klan. Nor did the play. But with the release of David Wark Griffith's movie *The Birth of a Nation*, thousands of moviegoers sat agog and stupefied. The flames of the second movement of the Ku Klux Klan ignited.

The *Birth of the Nation* movie portrays protagonist Klan Grand Dragon Ben Cameron and mounted followers saving white women from lusty Black men. Glorified vigilantism abounded, although in the 1920s, night riding was minimal. In the movie, the Klan targets saloons, roadhouses, gambling parlors, dance halls and prostitution. The two-hour, forty-five-minute epic film played to sell-out crowds. Initially, it was viewed by fifty million people. The project cost $110,000. It garnered $18 million in profits ($528 million in 2023). With the music by Wagner, such stars as Mae Marsh and Lillian Gish and battle scenes copied from the popular prints of Mathew Brady, Griffith produced a masterpiece.

It portrays realistic Civil War battle scenes. The story depicts destitute southern families during Sherman's march through the South. After the war is over, the solders return home. They find that northern Reconstruction has begun, and the Black people have become instruments of the carpetbaggers.

Birth of a Nation poster. *Courtesy of Charles Rambow Collection.*

Into this emotion-charged scene gallops the hooded Klansmen to rescue the fair damsel and the floundering South from complete degradation.

The final scene of the movie is unforgettable. The beautiful heroine is trapped. She's surrounded by lecherous Black men ready to break down the door of her cabin. A military bugle signals help is on the way. An orchestra intensifies the scene with fortissimo sounds of "In the Halls of the Mountain King."

The Klan is on its way. Does the heroine hear the galloping hooves? The scene pans back and forth.

The rescuing Klan and the menacing Black threat are soon to collide. Will the lovely one be violated?

Saved? The tension in the movie theater intensifies.

In cities of the old South, men leaped to their feet, yelled, whooped and cheered as the savior Klansmen arrived in time. There were some reports that members of the viewing audience got so agitated they literally pulled out guns and shot at the screen.

Professor Desmond Ang, assistant professor of public policy at Harvard Kennedy School, measured the brutally racist movie's responses. He measured lynchings, race riots and Ku Klux Klan recruitment in counties after it was shown. Ang concluded that from 1915 to 1919, the film incited significant increases in racial violence—roadshow counties were five times more likely to have a lynching or race riot and three times more likely to have a new Klan chapter after the movie was screened.

The movie became a massive cultural landmark in American history.

Dixon arranged a private showing for his former college mate President Woodrow Wilson. This was the first movie ever screened in the White House. It remains one of the highest-grossing movies of all times. It has been seen totally by an estimated two hundred million people. Wilson, a racist, was much moved by the movie. "It is like writing history with lighting," he remarked and then added, "My only regret is that it is so terribly true."

President Woodrow Wilson, classmate of Thomas Dixon, was profoundly impressed by a private viewing of *The Birth of a Nation*. He commented, "The world must be made safe for democracy....We are but one of the champions of the rights of mankind." *Courtesy of the Woodrow Wilson Presidential Library Museum.*

In the 1920s, the movie *Face at Your Window* was a typical media influence that helped play up the growing fears, anxieties and suspicions in America. With so much economic and political uncertainty, society could use anyone who had answers. *Public domain.*

Other movies, like *The Face at Your Window*, released on October 31, 1920, by Fox Film Corporation and *The Ku Klux Klan Rides Again* hit the screens. They provided additional ammunition to advance the fledgling Klan movement. Their showings, however, lacked the effect and popularity of *Birth of a Nation*.

The media played a key role in both the birth, rebirth and demise of the KKK. Not only did a blockbuster movie like *The Birth of a Nation* shape the thinking, imagination and behavior of the populace, but countless books, newspapers, magazines, posters, pamphlets and even cartoons evoked visceral responses as well.

Novels such as Thomas Dixon Jr.'s trilogy—*The Leopard's Spot* (1902), *The Clansman* (1905) and *The Traitor* (1907)—focused on Reconstruction from a southern perspective. Dixon depicts slavery as a boon to Black people by advancing them from "bondage and savagery into the light and strength of Christian civilization." But he also celebrated the end of slavery as necessary for the achievement of democracy and human brotherhood.

One sensational book published in 1836 fired up anti-Catholic sentiment for decades. *Awful Disclosures of Maria Monk or The Hidden Secret of a Nun's Life* claimed to expose the systematic sexual abuse of nuns, predatory priests and infanticide. The author, Maria Monk, spins a story about the nuns of the Religious Hospitallers of St. Joseph of Montreal Convent of Hôtel-Dieu. The imagined account presented like a firsthand observation tells of "Black Nuns" who were forced to have sex with the priests in the seminary next door. The predatory priests supposedly sneaked over to the nunnery via a secret tunnel. After having sex that produced a baby, the child was baptized and then strangled and dumped into a lime pit in the basement. Nuns who refused to comply suddenly disappeared.

The horrors and degradation of *Awful Disclosures* prompted Protestants, with the assistance of a local bishop in Montreal, to conduct an investigation. The investigation came to naught. No evidence whatsoever surfaced.

Monk claimed she had lived in the Hôtel-Dieu convent for seven years, became pregnant and fled because she did not want her baby killed.

Maria Monk possibly suffered a brain injury as a child according to some reports. She actually lived in an asylum for seven years. It was the Magdalen Asylum for Wayward Girls where she met a fellow patient who is mentioned in her book. When she first told her story, Protestant minister Reverend John Jay Slocum in New York encouraged and possibly assisted her to publish it. The *American Protestant Vindicator* reported total sales of twenty-six thousand copies by July 1936. Even though scholars labeled the book a hoax, it nonetheless continued to remain in print. Wherever and whenever there appears an atmosphere of anti-Catholic sensationalism, it is revived. At least two Australian editions appeared in 1920 and 1940. A facsimile edition was published in 1977.

This author remembers seeing a yellowed copy of *Awful Disclosures of Maria Monk* in my parents' home in the 1940s, though my sister and I do not recall how or by whom it was acquired.

The role *Awful Disclosures of Maria Monk* may have played to inflame anti-Catholicism hysteria during the second movement of the Ku Klux Klan is unknown, but it was certainly available.

A second anti-Catholic book was written by Helen Jackson, *Convent Cruelties,* or *My Life in a Convent.* It was published in 1919 and had seven editions between 1919 and 1924. The memoir recounts her entering her first Felician convent and the misery she endured. Jackson quickly realized that the nuns were not kind, unlike the enchanting nuns she had previously known. Instead, they were cruel and vindictive to their charges. They punished her for many indiscretions, from disobedience to questioning the nuns' authority. Jackson escaped, but another determined nun forced her back into the convent against her will by "punching, pinching and nearly pulling her to pieces."

The most important principle was liberty. Jackson asserted that the convent, a Catholic prison, blatantly ignored the founding ideal. She said she managed to escape with the help of her friend Vivian. Vivian Graeff, a Baptist, saved the girls by hiding them in her home.

Helen Jackson went on a lecture circuit, captivating audiences with tales of horror. She reported on infanticide that covered up priests' illicit relationships with nuns. Her comrade on the lecture circuit, L.J. King, wrote pamphlets and gave speeches on similar topics.

King's specialty emerged, denouncing the confessional, since women were made especially vulnerable and taken advantage of by the priest in that setting. To prove his claims, King used selections from other former nuns and priests, including ex-priest Charles Chiniquy and Maria Monk.

Between 1874 and 1875, Chiniquy wrote *The Priest, the Woman, and the Confessional,* which supposedly documents confessions he heard as a priest in Canada. Charles Chiniquy was eventually excommunicated by Bishop Duggan from Chicago. Yet L.J. King had the gall to selectively quote the disgraced Chiniquy as he continued to travel about promoting his lecture.

The careers of Helen Jackson and L.J. King thrived on the fears of the Catholic church.

However, the Catholic Church did not ignore the fabrications of Jackson, King, H.W. Evans, the Ku Klux Klan and other detractors. Authorities questioned the legitimacy of the narrative. The Catholic Church prepared a pamphlet titled *A Record of Anti-Catholic Agitators.* It revealed Jackson as a fake ex-nun. She actually was sent to the House of the Good Shepherd in Detroit because of her own misconduct. The misconduct included questionable behavior with young men.

King was exposed as a fake ex-priest. He was accused of assaulting a woman because she protested portions of his lectures. His records showed he had been arrested for riots and resisting arrest.[45]

Whatever their indiscretions were, both King and Jackson became popular with members of the Ku Klux Klan, who relished their writings and lectures. Their stories of terror and debauchery confirmed the Klan's dogmas about the threats against vulnerable white women and the all-American home.

The role and power of journalism is a mixed bag. The newspaper medium effectively recruited Ku Klux Klaners by the thousands but also hastened the Klan's decline and death.

In a blog post, Patrick Young cites the first instance of the Klan being mentioned in a national news source: October 18, 1868.[46]

On that day, both the *New York Tribune* and the *New York Times* published an article on the Klan that caught the eye of readers around the country. It carried a story of the murder of Orange Rhodes in Pulaski, Tennessee. The account was followed by a critique of the role and presence of this "new" organization called the Ku Klux Klan.

The *New York Evening World*, under editor Herbert Bayard Swope, began investigating the "Second KKK Social Movement," in the summer of 1921. As the Klan's salesforce of Kleagles spread out across the country, the nation began to take notice. News reports of hooded vigilantes inflicting punishment and terror shocked a somnolent populace.

The *New York World* reported four killings, one mutilation, one branding with acid, forty-one floggings, twenty-seven tar-and-feather parties, five kidnappings, forty-three individuals warned to leave town or otherwise threatened, fourteen communities threatened by posters, sixteen parades of masked men with warning placards.

Then the big scoop appeared September 6, 1921. The *New York World* ran a three-week front-page exposé of the Klan. For twenty-one days, a barrage aimed at the Klan's ideology, activities, hooded secrecy and propensity for violence hit dead center. Swope, one of the premier editors of the time, realized that the Klan was a national menace and needed to be exposed.

The *New York World*'s best reporter and rewrite men produced the copy. It was a sensation, as many Catholics, Jewish and Black readers, slapped in the face, followed the revolting revelations. The paper managed to get nearly every major New York politician on record in opposition to the Klan.

William Randolph Hearst's *New York American* hurried a copycat series to press.

By Thanksgiving 1921, Americans everywhere knew about the new Klan. Sparked by the outcry of what appeared to be the growing menace, a congressional hearing convened.

The *New York World* gained between 60,000 and 100,000 readers. Ironically, the Klan gained hundreds of thousands of new members as well.

According to Colonel Simmons, in rural America where folks are blatantly anti–New York, many joiners came into the Klan fold bringing the actual coupons clipped from the *World*. The effect of the newspaper as a communication medium about the Klan both crippled and advanced the organization depending on a variety of circumstances.

In January 1923, the Imperial Kloncilium, the governing body of the Knights of the Ku Klux Klan, ordered the creation of an official publication. The *Imperial Night Hawk* was born. The weekly ran during the peak of Klan membership, from 1923 to 1924. By the end of 1924, the editors of the *Imperial Night Hawk* claimed that 36,591 copies were printed each week, with subscriptions in all forty-eight states. Each Klansman gained access to a subscription when he became initiated into membership.

Another popular Klan weekly, *The Dawn: The Herald of a New and Better Day* (1922–1924), trumpeted a circulation of fifty thousand in 1923. Ten cents were charged per copy at the new stands.

There were additional news magazines, such as the *Fiery Cross*, an Indiana publication, and the *Official Bulletins of the Grand Dragons*, which was a series of regional bulletins that reported on local and national events.

The National Ku Klux Klan leadership then decided to create their own national monthly newspaper syndicate by replacing the *Imperial Night Hawk* with the name *Kourier*. By early 1925, the *Kourier* claimed a circulation of over one and a half million readers. It became one of the most widespread weekly publications in the United States. Although its main purpose was propaganda, it used a folksy approach: news of the world, politics, humor, cartoons, Klan happenings and then, for example, a blistering denunciation of Catholicism or a tirade against one of their pet peeves.

The *Christian Century*, a monthly magazine founded in 1884 representing mainline Protestantism, was one of many that opposed the *Kourier*'s view on white supremacy. One exchange between Dr. Glenn Frank, a contributor to the *Christian Century*, and the editor of the *Kourier* battled over the belief that one could not be Christian while holding racist ideology. In the February 1926 issue, the *Kourier* tersely responded in defense of its position, saying, "The Klan supported white supremacy and opposed the 'deluge of aliens.'"

In Minneapolis, *The Call of the North* was published in 1923–24. It advertised itself in the Indiana *Fiery Cross* of the December 14, 1923 issue as "A Voice of Militant Protestantism."

The *North Dakota American* appeared as the official paper of the Klan in that state. It emerged at Fargo in late spring of 1925 and survived until 1928.

The Klan confronted a generally hostile press. In 1921, as soon as the Klan began to attract attention, the *Omaha World-Herald* carried editorials condemning the Klan. J. Hyde Sweet of the *Nebraska City News*, in an editorial widely reprinted, charged that "the Klan surrounded itself with mystery, hokum and bunk."

Print media, books, magazines, newspapers, pamphlets, posters and even cartoons served to promote the Klan ideological message and mission. Print media also exposed the Klan and assisted in bringing a dagger to its throat and its eventual (near) extinction.

6

THE KKK INVADES SMALL TOWNS

(CANTON, BERESFORD, ETC.)

Here comes the Watkins man!

There's a gentle knock on the door. The door opens. "Come in." It's the local Watkins salesman. Friendly, well-tailored, a gentleman. The Watkins salesman, a regular, is the door-to-door peddler of spices, herbs and kitchen specialties unavailable at the local grocery store. It's rural South Dakota in the 1920s and '30s. The Watkins salesman opens up his array of items. There's vanilla extract, various spices, liniment and shoe polish. Mom, the customer, enjoys the chatter, news in the neighborhood and, of course, the products themselves. A half hour flies by. A sale is made. Watkins man and Mom are both satisfied by the interaction and transaction. They bid adieu, and the Watkins man goes on to the next house.

Around the 1920s and into the 1930s, another Watkins salesman type knocks on a South Dakota door. Under the guise of selling 100 percent Americanism, his intentions are less honorable.

The smiling salesman is a Kleagle. "I'm here to help. For ten dollars you may join our fraternal, patriotic defender of the flag, motherhood and morality." Sounds good. Questions are answered. The deal is made.

The Klan Kleagle recruiters, under the leadership of Edward Clarke and Elizabeth Tyler, garnered a phenomenal growth in numbers and wealth during the 1920s. To join the Ku Klux Klan, a candidate paid a ten-dollar klectoken or initiation fee. The Kleagle/recruiter kept four dollars.

The King Kleagle of the state realm got one dollar. The Grand Goblin who served as the regional domain head got fifty cents. Two dollars and fifty cents went back to the Imperial Kleagles, Clarke and Tyler in Atlanta. Then the final two dollars went to the Imperial Wizard Simmons, making him a wealthy man. This pyramid scheme style generated an incredible amount of money while growing the organization. In 1921, the national Klan had over 100,000 members and continued growing like Burmese pythons in the Everglades.

Klan historian Charles Rambow from Rapid City described in a *South Dakota Journal* for the South Dakota Historical Society how a Kleagle could line his pockets. "If a higher klectoken or initiation fee could be garnered then the initial recruiter could count on an even greater profit." The scheme worked.

Money rolled in. New members were expected to buy their robe, hood and regalia through the headquarters in Atlanta. Klan publication subscriptions were also purchased through headquarters.

In 1921, Kleagles began to swarm. They arrived from Iowa and Indiana, landing in Beresford, Canton and throughout southeastern South Dakota. As they swarmed, they recruited, collected fees and brayed against radicalism, corruption and the Nonpartisan League. (The Nonpartisan League emerged in 1915 in North Dakota. It' founder, Arthur C. Townley, former organizer for the Socialist Party of America, assembled farmers and merchants to rally on their behalf. The league advocated state control of mills, grain elevators, banks and other farm-related industries. They organized to reduce the power of corporate interests from Minneapolis, Minnesota, and Chicago, Illinois. The state manager for the Nonpartisan League, Tom Ayres, wired the South Dakota governor for protection from the Klan.)

The *Sioux Valley News* in Canton published this article on Thursday, April 3, 1921:

> *A Ku Klux Klan paper,* The Fiery Cross, *was distributed about the city sometime Thursday night. The more we hear of the Klan and their methods of flying by night the less we like them. That's the only newspaper we have ever heard of that has to be distributed under cover of darkness and the Klan is the only organization we know of that must get in their work after peace-loving and God fearing people have retired.*

An editorial from the *Sioux Valley News* dated Thursday, July 14, 1921, called for tolerance:

Watkins Almanac cover. J.R. Watkins Medical Co., Winona, MN, 1917. *Smithsonian Libraries and Archives.*

The Ku Klux Klan

Several papers in the state have commented on the Ku Klux Klan recently organized in South Dakota, and only a few have mentioned it in commendatory tones, while a great many have very much against the idea.... The Ku Klux Klan while they were organized did only the things that protected rather than to kill and tear away the foundation of the United States of America....It is necessary in South Dakota to have a Ku Klux Klan to keep the radicals from tearing away the foundation of the United States....If the Ku Klux Klan is a law abiding organization and is patriotic [sic] it should be left alone.

The June 11, 1924 issue of the *Fiery Cross* offered this glowing growing report:

CANTON HAS BIG GROWTH
Canton Klan Is Showing Very Rapid Growth During the Past Few Weeks

Canton, S. Dak.,—Canton can boast of about as rapid growth as any Klan in the state of South Dakota. During the past week there has been a couple of classes taken into the order and the work of organizing hereabouts has barely begun. For a long time the people here held back, mostly because they knew little or nothing about the order, but of late it seems to be the habit of most of them to seek ways of getting into the organization. It has been keeping the organizer busy to take care of all of the applicants for membership and help has had to be secured in a couple of instances.

The May 22, 1924 issue of Canton's *Sioux Valley News* and the May 29, 1924 issue of the *Beresford News* reported fire and explosions:

K.K.K. BURNS CROSS HERE
Bombs Also Explode as Men Leave Flaming Cross at Fifth and Milwaukee
LEFT FRIDAY ON NIGHT

The Ku Klux Klan burned it's first fiery cross in the city of Canton last Friday night. Residents were startled about eleven o'clock by the loud explosion of several bombs which brought them to windows and doors to see what was happening. The cross had been placed at the of Fifth and Milwaukee streets where it burned brightly for several minutes. Neighbors who first saw the flames report seeing two men hurriedly enter a car and after the enemies of Americanism began pressure to bear from one side and Mrs. Hughes brought pressure from the other side, insisting that approval of the Japanese exclusion clause would seriously hamper diplomatic and commercial relations with Japan.

That the present Congress is the greatest in the history of the world was proven on frequent occasions during the past few months. These patriotic congressmen and senators proved to the world that they hold Americanism above everything and that when the question of Americanism and devotion to the flag is at stake party ties are of a secondary consideration.

Resisted Great Pressure

Wall street, foreign governments religios and alien interests of every description brought every pressure to bear upon Congress to force it to desert Americanism for capitalism and hyphenism, but to no avail. The little band of patriots on "The Hill" stood off the onslaughts of the combined enemies of Americanism and deserted party ties without hesitation and went down the line for Americanism.

The temper of Congress burst forth when it cast aside party alignments and passed the soldier's bonus and then repassed it over the President's veto in the face of a flood of telegrams from Wall Street and its agents scattered all over the country.

(Continued on page four)

OUTLINES EDUCA-
TIONAL POLICY

Imperial Wizard Outlines Education Policy of Klan in Raleigh Speech.

Raleigh, N. C.—More than 2,000 men and women were present at the city auditorium when Dr. W. Evens, imperial wizard, of the Ku Klux Klan, spoke on education and other related subjects. Dr. Evans was introduced to the audience by Judge Henry A. Grady, grand dragon of North Carolina. Bursts of applause greeted the remarks of Dr. Evans, as he outlined the policies of the Ku Klux Klan, through the organization was not mentioned by name.

At a meeting of the Raleigh Klan, Dr. Evans addressed several hundred delegates, when matters of importance to the organization was discussed. These two meetings are expected to have a great effect on the growth of the Klan in Raleigh and vicinity, intense enthusia will soon be among the leaders of the organized states.

Canistota, S. Dak.—The National speaker visited here again on Thursday evening of this week, and spoke to a much larger audience than previously. Not only was the audience larger but it was more enthusiastic and more real interest in the organization was shown.

After the talking by the National speaker, the doors were thrown open and candidates for admission into the order accepted. As before a large class answered the call with the difference that the class taken in on Thursday evening was quite a little larger than the previous class.

The Klan in McCook county and especially in Canistota, is growing rapidly and soon it will have swept the entire county.

CANTON KLAN
HAS BIG GROWTH

Canton Klan is Showing Very Rapid Growth During the Past Few Weeks

Canton, S. Dak.—Canton can boast of about as rapid growth as any Klan in the state of South Dakota.

During the past week there has been a couple of classes taken into the order and the work of organizing hereabouts has barely begun. For a long time the people here held back, mostly because they knew little or nothing about the order, but of late it seems to be the habit of most of them to seek ways of getting into the organization.

It has been keeping the organizer busy to take care of all of the applicants for membership and help has had to be secured in a couple of instances.

SPECTACULAR
CEREMONIAL

Jersey Klansmen and Klanswomen Hold Spectacular Ceremonial

Perhaps the largest gathering of Klansmen and Klanswomen which has been held in south Jersey to date, assembled Monday night, April 28th, at Bridgeton, N. J., in Klonklove and naturalized over five hundred candidates into their respective organizations of Cumberland county.

The crowd was so enormous that it took the guards and caretakers (continued on page three)

Special Investigators who have been investigating the report published in New Jersey neswpapers that during a recent ceremonial held at Spotswood, N. J., Klansmen had threatened to destroy the Jewish Synagogue at that place, have reported that no such warning had been issued by the Klansmen assembled. The report of the Investigator is also backed by a petition of twelve of the Jewish citizens of Spotswood demanding of the Perth Amboy Evening News the source of their information and denying fully that they had ever received a threat from the Klansmen.

At the time the Klan began to assemble at Spotswood according to the published report a prayer meeting was being held at the Synagogue and the Jews, continuing (Continued on Page four)

WILLISTON KLAN
TAKES IN CLASS

Large Class Taken in Here and Prospect Good for More to Follow

Williston, N. Dak.,—A large class was taken into the Klan here recently and from the present out look there will be another and larger one to be taken in in the near future.

There was quite a little opposition at the start owing to most of the people hereabouts knowing nothing about the Klan, its aims and ideals, but of late this opposition has vanished and the Klan is going right through like a whirlwind through a brush heap.

BOMERANGS
TO PERIODICALS

Exposes of Klan are Bomerangs to Periodicals

Almost every day in the week the press of the United States is giving some valuable information to the world on the activities of the Knights of the Ku Klux Klan. In (Continued on page three)

"Canton Has Big Growth" article. *From the* Fiery Cross, *June 11, 1924.*

drive away. Upon examination it was learned that the cross was about ten feet high. It was hinged in three places so that the cross arms could be folded up and another fold made in the center, thus making it easy to carry in a car. The cross also had a folding platform which it stood in the road.

The August 28, 1924 issue of Canton's *Sioux Valley News* front-page article featured a big Klan rally:

KU KLUX KLAN TO CELEBRATE
Affair to be staged at Edge of Canton Saturday Afternoon and Evening
INITIATES NEW MEMBERS

One of the largest crowds ever witnessed in Canton is expected on Saturday, when the Ku Klux Klan who hold their first public celebration in Canton. Everything has been arranged and the stage is set for a full demonstration of their ritual. Bands will contribute to the entertainment Nation and State speakers will be present to explain the cause of their being and the purpose of their existence. Speaking will start at 2:30 in the afternoon. Refreshments will be served on the grounds. The evening ceremony will begin promptly at 7:30 and will consist of public initiatory services, where it is expected that the ceremonies of initiation will be exemplified with a large number of candidates, after which a display of fireworks is promised.

According to the Thursday April 2, 1925 *Sioux Valley News*, the Ku Klux Klan had big plans:

CONTEMPLATE ERECTION OF $25,000 BLDG
Lincoln County Ku Klux Klan Considering Erection of Modern Clavern

The Lincoln County Ku Klux Klan have under consideration themselves the purchase of a corner located on South Cedar and Sixth Streets upon which they are anticipating the erection of a $25,000.00 two story modern clavern in which to conduct their meetings and other business. The building will comprise offices and a large hall. One of their head men will be in Canton this week and expects to locate here permanently. Upon his arrival here a large meeting will be held and definite arrangements will be made regarding the purchase of the site and the drawing of the plans for the erection of the building. The Klan has grown to such as enormous extent in county Lincoln that it was found necessary to have headquarters here.

In southeast South Dakota, the Ku Klux Klan continued to advance and grow. The *Beresford Republic* printed a warning letter on page 5 from F.D. Stedman on Thursday, May 21, 1925:

Effect of Ku Klux Klan on California Is Bad Says Stedman
Former Beresford Man Does Not Believe This Community Should "Indulge"

Friends—The Republic *reached me this morning as usual and I note with interest your article on the Klan....A beautiful little city 26 miles from here—Anaheim, California, a place of some 8,000 or so people in the very cream of Southern California has been the battle ground of Klan and anti-Klan forces for two years now and the effect has been truly terrible. First the Klan was in the saddle and got into power and Klansmen held all the city offices, all policemen were Klansmen, innocent people were persecuted because they were not members. Old friends became bitterest enemies. Merchants were boycotted and everything happened that could happen to disrupt the community. Last fall a recall election was held and all the Klansmen were thrown out after a fierce battle at the polls and conditions are a little bit better now.*

Yesterday I was there visiting Mrs. Stedman's two brothers and sister who live there and a certain preacher who was said to be the Cyclops of the Klan was holding services in a church guarded by the whole force of police. Sunday morning a hangman's noose was hung by his door nob [sic] while he was at church. Saturday he was assaulted and beaten on the street etc. In a place like Beresford the effect of a reign of terror like this one would certainly be a calamity and I hope there will be no Klan organized there. In this city there are thousands of Klansmen but I don't think they do a great deal of good or harm here. My own notion is that the organization while they have high sounding principles is entirely unnecessary and undesirable. With kindest regards to my friends at Beresford.
Respectively,
F.D. Stedman

On October 27, 1921, the *Huron Evening Huronite* carried this story:

S.D. FARMER IS THREATENED BY KU KLUX KLAN

Alcester, S.D., October 27.—Apparently an imitation of the Ku Klux Klan has invaded South Dakota.

One night recently about 15 masked and armed men called on Les Morlan, a wealthy farmer living about five miles southwest of Alcester, and demanded that he return to Harry Hampton, a tenant on one of his farms some rent notes, which Morlan is alleged to have refused to surrender a short time previous when he sold out Hampton on a sheriffs sale.

Morlan saw the masked figures from his upstairs window and refused to come out whereupon they entered the house carrying on a conversation through the closed bedroom door. Morlan, not having the rent notes in the house, agreed to produce them within 48 hours upon threats from the gang of masked men to "string him to a telephone pole and fill him full of lead."

The unwelcome visitors departed as silently as they came.

From the *Fiery Cross*, May 28, 1924 edition, Elk Point KKK activity was reported:

Opposition at Elk Point Strong
Elk Point Klan Is Making Good Progress in Spite of the Strong Roman Element

Elk Point, S.D.,—The Elk Point Klan met recently and took in a fair sized class all things considered.

When it comes to opposition it is the opinion of Klansmen here that it is stronger in this part of the state than in any other. The Roman element here is very thick and they are leaving no stone unturned to make the organization of the Klan a failure.

In a sense this is only stimulating the boys to harder work and making the ones on the outside more anxious to become affiliated with the movement.

The Ku Klux Klan expanded to Worthing in South Dakota, as indicated in a local paper dated Thursday, June 11, 1925: "The Ku Klux Klan held an organization meeting here [Worthing, S.D.] Wednesday evening."

From the *Fiery Cross* of May 28, 1924, this article championed Canistota Klan resilience and attentiveness to the national KKK speaker.

Canistota Klan Holds Meeting
Muddy Roads and Threatening Weather Has No Terror for People Around Canistota

Canistota, S.D.,—In spite of the muddy condition of the roads as a result of a heavy rain of the preceding night, a large crowd turned out to hear the National Lecturer in the interests of the Ku Klux Klan.

For over two hours the speaker held his audience and they were sorry when he had finished his discourse.

After the speaking the cards that were signed up and turned in gave evidence of the interest taken in the Klan in this vicinity.

From the *Fiery Cross,* June 11, 1924, this article touted growth in Canistota and McCook County.

CANISTOTA KLAN AT IT ONCE MORE
National Speaker Visits Canistota for the Second Time in a Month

Canistota, S.D.,—The National Speaker visited here again on Thursday evening of this week and spoke to a much larger audience than previously. Not only was the audience larger but it was more enthusiastic and more interest in the organization was shown. After talking by the National Speaker, the doors were thrown open and candidates for admission were accepted. As before a large class answered the call with the difference that the class taken in on Thursday evening was quite a little larger than the previous class. The Klan in McCook County and especially in Canistota is growing rapidly and soon it will have swept the entire county.

1

SLITHERING INTO
SIOUX FALLS

In the dead of night in July 1921, an investigative reporter from the *Sioux Falls Press* ascends up the back stairs of the Sioux Falls Carpenter Hotel. His purpose: to rendezvous with a man who claims to have no name. The Carpenter Hotel, a landmark structure founded in 1912 at 221 Phillips Avenue, is handy for such private clandestine meetings. Once the reporter reaches the landing, he turns and walks down the dimly lit hall. His eye searches for a certain room number. His role, he rehearses, is to meet and wrestle information out of this mystery man. He finds the room, knocks and waits. No answer. Knocks again.

"Who is it?"

"A reporter from the *Sioux Falls Press*."

"Come in."

The reporter, almost apologetically, introduces himself. The mystery resident of the room greets the reporter and then quickly explains, "I am known by no other name than King Kleagle." (All Kleagles are sworn not to reveal their names by order of the very Imperial Wizard, Colonel William J. Simmons from Atlanta, Georgia, Grand Commander of the National Klan, including South Dakota.)

The inquiry begins. The reporter, cautious at first, presses for information. King Kleagle speaks. A veil of secrecy begins to lift. What the reporter would learn, on this the first public announcement of the purpose of the Klan in South Dakota, is a version of pseudo-patriotism and Americanism mixed with Protestant theology.

The reporter listens. His pen flies. Scribbles wildly as King Kleagle describes the reason for the new Klan in South Dakota: "We are organized as an active American association of true American men" (as recorded in the *Sioux Falls Press* and later in the July 7, 1921 *Beresford Republic*). "We are opposed to radicalism; we believe in white supremacy as fundamentally right. Our membership is limited to people born in America. We believe in the Protestant religion and all who place the United States of America above any other form of government in the world."

"Are you then a political force?" the *Sioux Falls Press* reporter interrupts. King Kleagle continues, "The purpose of the Klan is only to drive out radicals

The Sioux Falls Carpenter Hotel at 221 South Philips, circa 1912.
Public domain.

out of American life by legal process and not by intimidation and to do all in it's power to make active Americanism the greatest thing in this nation....We have no fight with organized labor....The Klan is opposed to the Nonpartisan League....We believe in and will support the free public system...and we believe in and fight for free speech and free press....Most of all we believe in and will protect the home and chastity of American womanhood."

"Are there charter organizations in Sioux Falls?" reporter asks. "Already here in Sioux Falls," King Kleagle replies, "dozens of prominent business and professional men and members of organized labor have come...and signified their intention of joining the Klan."

King Kleagle admits, "Last night in my room here in the Carpenter Hotel several prominent businessmen, most of them members of the American Legion conferred with me. I am confident that within one week the organization will be perfected here with a membership of at least 500." Next question, "What is your plan of action?"

"One of the first publicity measures to be taken by the Klan will be a showing at a local theater in the near future of two pictures, one, *The Face at Your Window*, an attack upon radicalism and an exposition of it's danger, and secondly, *The Ku Klux Klan Rides Again*. There will be no night-riding, no white-capped assaults upon the peace and property of citizens. That much is sworn. There will be no revelation of the members or the nature of their plans. That much is also sworn."

"Well sir, what is your name? How can I know who you are?" the reporter bluntly asks.

"The only key to my identity—the only way by which those like you desiring information can reach me and other Kleagles or lieutenants, is by addressing post office box #562."

The interview, now past midnight, ends abruptly. A final admonition: "Whoever you talk to you must swear to tell only what I, King Kleagle, have told you for publicity. Good bye and good night."

Down the back steps of the Carpenter Hotel, a satisfied reporter— notebook crammed in hand—scurries out into the darkness. Later, back at his desk, an unnerving story unfolds:

THE KU KLUX KLAN IN SOUTH DAKOTA
Organization Calculated to Reduce Radicalism in State

Out of the years of decay, rising Phoenix-like from the ashes of 50 years ago, the Klan has come again—for this time no carpetbaggers, no efforts for blacks to hold their place in society rather than an attempt to ride to equality with the white man—this time rather, say it's members, in solemn conference right here in Sioux Falls, for war to the knife on radicalism and disbelievers in Americanism.

The July 21, 1921 issue of the *Beresford Republic* paper then reported that the *Argus Leader* wired Imperial Wizard Simmons as follows: "Is there a bona fide agent of the Ku Klux Klan working under your supervision organizing a chapter of the organization? Some local people express doubts as to his authenticity. He styles himself as Kleagle." Simmons wired back a quick reply:

The Ku Klux Klan has several representatives in Sioux Falls. Reports emanating from Sioux Falls that this organization is formed to fight South Dakota farmers is a contemptible falsehood. It is a legally chartered patriotic and fraternal organization. It stands uncompromisingly for impartial enforcement of all laws and stands ready at any and all times to assist if called upon in aiding properly constituted authorities in suppressing outbreaks against law and order. It is the duty of all Klans men to lend their moral and physical help to all movements tending to the betterment of interests of community state and nation....Only 100 per cent Americans are eligible for membership... [Signed] W.J. Simmons, Imperial Wizard, Knights of the Ku Klux Klan.

A *Madison Daily Leader* article of July 9, 1921, "KU KLUX KLAN IS NOT ANTAGONISTIC," attempted to clarify the tension between the Ku Klux Klan and the Nonpartisan League. Tom Ayres, manager of the Nonpartisan League, wired Governor McMaster asking that the league be investigated, claiming that the new organization was threatening the league and peaceful citizens. King Kleagle, Klan organizer in South Dakota, responded, "We do not expect to fight the Nonpartisan League, we are simply opposed to it's policies."

The surprise growth of the Ku Klux Klan in the 1920s erupted into a nationwide phenomenon. It engulfed most every community. From Indiana and Iowa, Kleagle Klansmen came trotting into Sioux Falls. They organized a first Ku Klux Klavern in the spring of 1921. The Klan members spouted being pro-American, pro-Gentile, pro-white and Protestant. They railed against anarchists, radicals, enemies of the public schools, submitters to the foreign pope and every alien enemy of America.

Organized prejudice, hate speech and intolerance sprouted like leafy spurge in virgin grassland.

How the Kleagles ignited this wildfire growth is no mystery. The Ku Klux Klan simply exploited the appearance of threat—real or imagined. In every community, the Kleagles found out the most pressing need or worry. Concentrating on that threat, they made sure the Klan was viewed as the only savior and protector.

There were a lot of issues to stoke fear. Postwar depression idled many workers. Immigrants were flooding the country. Easily, the Klan sowed in the minds of many the seeds for anti-immigration, anti-Catholic, anti-Jews, anti-Asian, fear of lawlessness and prevalence of societal curses as blatant bootlegging and general moral decline.

Not everyone embraced the Ku Klux Klan out of fear. An editorial in the *Beresford Republic* from July 7, 1921, leaned openly, cautiously and favorably for the Ku Klux Klan:

> *An article printed elsewhere in this paper taken from the* Sioux Falls Press, *tells of an organization of a Ku Klux Klan in South Dakota. We do not know if the report is authentic, or the imaginations of a reporter and while the principle of the well known "Klan" are not perfect the purposes announced are so thoroughly American that we cannot pass them up unnoticed. The elimination of the radical who is aiming to overthrow our form of government, the perpetuating of the public school system, the declaration that while free speech and free press are fundamental principles in our government, yet people who are openly talking and writing against our government and seeking it's overthrow should be taken in charge. These and other questions are grave ones and if the "Klan" can be composed of men of high standing it would wield an influence. It is a matter, however, that should be backed by the best of judgment.*

By 1922, Ku Klux Klaverns had been established in over twenty South Dakota towns. It soon blossomed to over one thousand members.

The *Minnesota Fiery Cross*, an official paper of the Klan, which replaced the *Call of the North*, on July 27, 1923, carried this border state article from Friday, March 7, 1924:

> *Dakota Town Startled by Burning of Fiery Cross*
> *Symbols of Klan seen in all sections of Sioux Falls, following explosions of aerial bombs and star shells. Residents call police and newspaper offices.*

(Special Correspondence)

Sioux Falls, S.D., March 1—There is no mistaking the fact in this city today, that the Knights of the Ku Klux Klan are here.

Thursday night, the organization made it's presence known in no uncertain way. Bombs and star shells were exploded in the air, and fiery crosses were set ablaze simultaneously in all parts of the city. It was not until after 10 o'clock that the community was startled by the first bomb, followed by many others, and divers star shells.

A cross was soon seen burning on the North Minnesota Avenue hill and another at Minnesota Ave and fourth street. Near the east side Cemetery another symbol of the Klan was discovered by startled residents and in the eastern side of the city, near Cherry Rock Bridge, a fourth cross was flaming. Local newspaper offices, police and fire departments received many telephone calls from startled citizens asking, "What was the explosion?" Later it was learned that the explosions were only announcements of the burning of the crosses which were seen in all sections.

The Press *here as in other places, where the Klan has started, attacks the organization, endeavoring to paint a picture of it as a lawless band of outlaws.*

Sioux Falls Coliseum at 515 North Main. *Public domain.*

In September 1924, local members of the Ku Klux Klan made a decision to conduct a large meeting supposedly to conduct informative lecture(s). They requested the use of the Sioux Falls Coliseum. The purpose of the lecture(s) would be to inform the public about the KKK. When the public got wind of this request, a group formed to confront Mayor Thomas McKinnon. The protesting group included John Cogley, T.M. Bailey, Richard Bielski, Tom Kirby, Michael Luddy, Frank Gallagher, Charles H.D. Mitchell, C.C. Caldwell, Holton Davenport, Sam Speier, George McDonald and twenty to twenty-five others. However, Mayor Thomas McKinnon had already approved the request, seeing they were local taxpayers.

The Sioux Falls Klavern of the KKK also requested permission for a grand parade in downtown Sioux Falls in the fall of 1924. Sioux Falls mayor McKinnon and the chief of police approved the parade permit provided all participants walked unmasked. On September 28, 1924, the parade began. Five hundred Klansmen in white robes, hoods and masks—some riding horses covered with white sheets—marched in the downtown area. The vast crowd of local citizenry, wide-eyed, watched the Klansmen march two abreast with arms folded on their chests. They walked south down Main Avenue to Twelfth Street, east to Phillips Avenue, north to Eighth Street and then west to Minnesota Avenue.

However, the Klansmen in the parade violated the stipulations of the permit—that no one would wear masks. So as a result, many parade watchers ridiculed the Klansmen because they insisted on hiding their identities. After the parade, the Klansmen met for ceremonies near where present-day Lyon Park is located. Several scores of initiates joined as new members.

An eight-foot-tall pole with a wooden crossbar attached was planted on the hill. The cross, wrapped in burlap soaked in a flammable substance, lit up the neighborhood.[47]

The *Argus Leader* June 5, 1928 issue reported a divided decision on a Ku Klux Klan request to rent the Coliseum:

Regular Meeting

The Board of Commissioners of the City of Sioux Falls met in regular session on Monday, June 4, 1928 at 9 o'clock a. m. With the following members present at roll call: Commissioners, Joseph S. Nelson and Alex Reid and Mayor Thomas McKinnon. All members present…

An application was received from the Ku Klux Klan for permission to hold a free public meeting in the Coliseum on the evening of June 5, 1928, at 8 o'clock. The application was granted on motion by the following vote on roll call: Yeas: Nelson, Reid, 2. Nays, Mr. Mayor, 2.

According to the May 12, 1927 *Sioux Falls Argus Leader*, the Klan planned to grow:

KLAN BUYS LAND FOR GATHERINGS
Ten Acre Plot East of City Purchased at Price Given as $3,000

Purchase of ten acres of ground east of the city on which open air meetings may be held this summer was announced today by Klan 16, realm of South

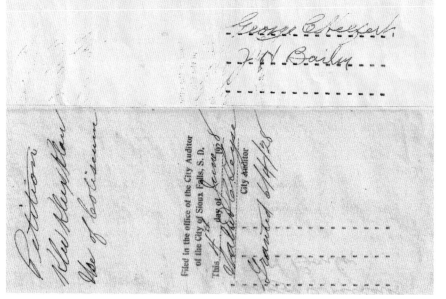

Local Sioux Falls Klavern application request for venue usage to city council. *Courtesy Jim Carlson Collection.*

Dakota, Knights of the Ku Klux Klan. The land is about a half mile east of the state school for the deaf and has formerly been used occasionally by the organization....

This is the fourth location of the Klan in its life the past three years in Sioux Falls. When first organized in the spring of 1924 the hooded members had a ceremonial on a farm southeast of the city, about a half mile beyond the Cherry Rock bridge.

Next they were holding meetings about four miles west of the city on the Twelfth Street road, and afterwards north of the county farm, about four miles north of the city. Still later they were found on their present location.

An article in the *Argus Leader*, preserved on Newspaper.com, carried this Sunday, October 19, 1930 news:

CROSS BURNED NEAR CATHOLIC CATHEDRAL
Believed by Police to Be Work of Klan; Placed Before Officials' Residence

[A] burning cross, thought by police to have been placed by members of the Ku Klux Klan was discovered burning on a sidewalk near St. Joseph's Cathedral early this morning. The cross was situated before the residence occupied by church officials. Police officers, investigating a report of a fire, discovered the blazing emblem. It was about five feet high and two feet wide and is said to have been wrapped in kerosene soaked burlap. Officers scouted a theory that the cross was the work of boys, declaring that it showed evidence of immature craftsmanship.

As the Ku Klux Klan slithered into Sioux Falls, its contagious influence spread to the surrounding towns. One hot Saturday evening in July 1924, farmers came to Dell Rapids to sell their cream and eggs and to shop. Neighbors gathered on sidewalks and in businesses, chatted leisurely about family, politics and the crops. Teens enjoyed renewed friendships as they sat at the drugstore fountain counter sipping cherry cokes and malted milks. It was an unusually large crowd, with both sides of the business streets lined with parked cars.

No one noticed seven or eight automobiles coast to a silent stop on a dimly lit side street. Fifty Klansmen dressed in white robes, pointed hoods and masks got out of the cars and began to organize.

Suddenly, they appeared in an orderly procession at about ten o'clock, parading down Main Street.

Photo of sixty masked and hooded members of the Sioux Falls Ku Klux Klan. The honor guard flanks the main road leading into Woodlawn Cemetery for the burial of one of their fellow Klansmen. *Courtesy of Owner Lore Tucker.*

Ku Klux Klan Konvocation near Sioux Falls. *Courtesy of Lore Tucker.*

They passed slowly through the congested traffic. The crowd watched with absorbing interest, speculating where they came from and what their intent was. Silently, with no music or speechmaking, they walked. And then they disappeared.

The August 1, 1924 *Dell Rapids Tribune News* speculated that the bootleggers in the area had been given a warning about the Klan:

> *It is said that one of the most active bootleggers, accompanied by his wife, had his car with a supply of moonshine just around the corner from Fourth Street on LaDell Street, and is alleged to have dispensed earlier in the evening, while his wife sat in the car, but it appeared that he had exhausted his stock and got away before the Klansmen made their appearance. It is said that he has carried on quite extensive bootlegging operations in Dell Rapids recently, without interference on the part of local officers, and, after the parade of the Klan there was some speculation as to whether the Klansmen would have taken any action against him in case they had arrived a little earlier and caught him at his bootlegging.*
>
> *From all the reports of the bootlegging that is going on in Dell Rapids it would seem that the federal, state and county officers might be able to make a worth-while raid here some Saturday night, which it appears to be made the occasion for a general supply of moonshine.*

Earlier on Wednesday March 12, 1924, the *Argus Leader* published this article:

> *SEND WARNINGS TO BOOTLEGGERS*
> *Suspected Operators at Dell Rapids Get Letters Telling Them To Stop Activities*
>
> *Dell Rapids, March 12.—The Ku Klux Klan has effected an organization here, or unknown persons are posing as members of the Klan, for during the past week a number of crosses have been burned in this immediate vicinity.*
>
> *This may have been the work of jokesters, but several suspected bootleggers do not think there is a joke about warning letters they have received, telling them to cease their illegal traffic in liquor or suffer the consequences.*
>
> *It is said the bootleggers are inclined to take a serious view of the warnings, so there is a possibility that in the future less moonshine liquor will be in evidence in Dell Rapids and vicinity.*

In the broader Sioux Valley area, thirty miles southwest of Sioux Falls, the Ku Klux Klan had already made inroads by 1924. Parker, South Dakota, gained notoriety by an article in the *Mitchell Evening Republican* on April 17:

> *FLEEGER WARNED TO STICK TO THE LAW; THINKS LETTER IS JOKE*
> *Parker, S.D., April 17.—Judge L.L. Fleeger, one of the circuit court judges for the Second Judicial District, and a resident of Parker, received a communication alleged to be from the Ku Klux Klan, threatening him to be very diligent and to stick to the letter of the law in sentencing malefactors, big or little. The letter was dated April 1 and mailed from Sioux Falls. Judge Fleeger thinks that the communication may be an April Fool's joke, rather than Klan material.*
>
> *The K.K.K., however, seems to be quite active in Turner county lately, or else some individuals are having a great deal of fun at the people's expense.*
>
> *A cross was burned at Chancellor recently and also one at Davis, both of which towns are located in the eastern part of the county.*

8

THE KKK SPREADS ACROSS SOUTH DAKOTA

One May night in 1924, three bombs exploded in sleepy Mitchell, South Dakota. The blasts preceded three hastily constructed burlap-wrapped timber crosses, which in turn burst into mini infernos. The first bomb went off at about 9:30 p.m. The second and third bombs followed fifteen minutes later. The second explosion was by far the most powerful of the three and rattled houses on the west side of Mitchell. The bombs' blasts and the scary sight of burning fiery crosses shocked the townsfolk. Many knew, however, that the local Klan was up to their shenanigans. Yet how wise was this display of presence and bravado just when the KKK needed support for its most recent request?

One of the premier sites for multiple venues taking place in South Dakota is the famous Corn Palace in Mitchell. The present palace building, conceived as a gathering place to celebrate the climax of the crop growing season and harvest, was built in 1921. It offered city residents and rural neighbors multiple opportunities to enjoy a fall festival with an assortment of stage entertainments. The palace is redecorated each year with naturally colored corn, other grains and native grasses. Twelve different colors or shades of corn are used. It has become "the agricultural show-place of the world."[48] It has played host to industrial exhibits, dances, stage shows, meetings, banquets, proms, athletic events and now, in 1924, a request for a large Ku Klux Klan confab.

The *Mitchell Evening Republican* reported on May 8 the discussion of the special KKK request:

The Mitchell Corn Palace in 1924. *Courtesy of Donna Weiland, Mitchell, South Dakota.*

The question of permitting the Klan to use the Corn Palace for a meeting place tonight was to be decided this afternoon by the city council. At the request for the use of the building night, H.D. Brown, an organizer of the Klan, was told that the council would consider renting the Corn Palace to the Klan providing ten property owners in the city would sign a request for the use of the building.

This morning this petition was presented to the city auditor and Mayor J.E. Williams immediately issued a call for a special meeting of the council.

Special meeting of the council incited a big "no" to the KKK request. The spacious Corn Palace would be off-limits. "Why?" many asked. Then what happened? The stern council rebuff unleashed a mighty backlash.

In a front-page column, the *Fiery Cross* boasted this stunning rebound on May 28, 1924:

*MEMBERS COMING IN SO FAST AT MITCHELL—CAN GET NO REST
THE MITCHELL KLAN REPORTS THE INCREASE IN MEMBERSHIP SO GREAT THAT THE ORGANIZER HAS LITTLE TIME FOR REST
Recent Action of the City Council in Refusing the Use of the Corn Palace Resulted in Fair Minded People Taking the Part of the Klan*

Mitchell, S.D.,—With the organizers in Mitchell, the problem of how to reach the red-blooded American citizens has been solved, but with the solution of one another rises that demands quick action and ready hands. For with a steady stream pouring in and out of the office daily, the question now confronting the organizers is: How to handle the crowd.

It's been suggested that a den of skunks placed in the doorway which would not only give the organization a chance to catch up with their work, but the smoke of the battle would be an inspiration, to all prospective klansmen reminding that of the fact that the fight for free schools, just laws and liberty demands strong minds, great hearts, true faith and ready hands…and the Klansmen are not Klanish when it comes to the protection of pure womanhood for they will protect the Mothers and Daughters of this country…against the brothel, the white slaves, the junket-peddler, the needle-pusher and all acts that are in any way questionable.

Are you with us Mothers and Daughters? If so, get that husband and sweetheart of yours to seek out the Klavern of the Ku Klux Klan and there beneath the Fiery Cross, which is emblematically of the cross on which your Saviour died burning up the sins and dross of the world. He will receive a vision, that will lift him, upon a higher plane of citizenship with more respect for our Constitution and Flag under whose protection the Gospel of Jesus Christ will be permitted to Live, and not be crushed out by the Beast and the false prophets. And if the sight of Old Glory and Free Public schools are nauseating, too, any citizen of this good old U S.A. I know of no more pleasing sight, too many optics, than to see them on board with her nose pointing across the Atlantic and as she leaves the American shore, you will find me climbing the Statue of Liberty with the Bible in one hand and Old Glory in the other, and reaching the highest point you will hear this glad refrain striking the America shore: "Praise God! From whom all blessing flow." [This column from the KKK official newspaper in a rambling way mixes Christianity and patriotism, much like mixing a can of soup with a cake mix. One gets *caoup*, similar to civil religion.]

When shots were fired at Lake Byron, twenty-two miles north of Huron, the sportsmen in the area had had enough. According to the *Madison Daily Leader*, poachers had been shooting at ducks and geese with high-powered rifles. Every year this happened. The local hunters decided to organize into a vigilante group "similar to the Ku Klux Klan to put a stop to this violation of the state game laws." (Wherever the appearance of lawlessness happened in South Dakota, the Ku Klux Klan offered to provide law and order).

According to the *Miller Press*, by March 20, 1924, the Ku Klux Klan had invaded Huron. They actively organized a klavern and burned a cross at 11:20 p.m. in the heart of the city, at the old Elks lot on Third Street at the corner of Ohio Avenue. Crosses were also burned near the packing plant, near the cemetery. Then, as reported in the *Huron Evening Huronite*, on June 24, 1924,

> *practically every automobile in Huron was parked to the south of the Packing Plant...where the Ku Klux Klan was holding an initiation.... Bombs announced the approaching ceremonies, while sheeted and hooded figures could be seen in the pasture shortly before sundown. With the cross lighting up the immediate surrounding areas with a weird light augmented by pretty flares of red glows...the novices were given the fundamental patriotic principles which it is known the Ku Klu Klan advances. Three crosses were burned during the evening while 250 men joined the Klan. It was estimated that somewhere between 1,000 and 1,500 klansmen participated standing in the semi-circle.*

An *Argus Leader* carried news of a first Huron event on October 18, 1924:

> *Men dressed in the white hoods and robes of the Knights of the Ku Klux Klan numbering 50, attended the funeral services of R.B. Knight here yesterday afternoon in the Congregational church. This was the first public funeral held in Huron at which members of the "invisible empire" appeared in regalia. Masons, Odd Fellows, Modern Woodman and members of the railroad brotherhoods to which Mr. Knight belonged, also attended the service in a body. At the graveside where the Masonic services were conducted, the klansmen formed a circle outside the Masonic circle at the grave while one of the hooded trumpeters sounded "Taps."*

The women of Huron also joined the klan. According to the *Huron Evening Huronite* on February 10, 1925, "the women of the Ku Klux Klan burned their second cross west of the city Saturday night."

In some communities, the invasion of the Ku Klux Klan was met with fierce resistance. In Gettysburg, South Dakota, in February 1923, a vigorous campaign against the Klan was launched when J.H. Williams, commander of the American Legion, issued a call to support his actions. He opposed the Klan and said he knew there were members of the legion who are also members of the Klan. It was time to weed them out: "I feel, however, that the loss in quantity of members…will mean a corresponding increase in quality."

A fiery cross was ignited at Wylie Park in Aberdeen on August 10, 1923. That night 350 clansmen gathered for ceremonies. Aberdeen and Brown County claimed a large Ku Klux Klan presence: 35 candidates joined. One Klansman stated that he and three other Aberdonians became members of the Klan in Chicago and had been commissioned to develop a Klan organization here in the Hub City of Aberdeen.

The *Frederick Free Press* carried this news article on August 14, 1924:

The Ku Klux Klan Meet at Aberdeen

The Clan meeting at Aberdeen last Friday night drew what is estimated to be the largest crowd ever assembled in the north half of the state if not in the entire state. Long before the scheduled time for the speaking to commence almost a steady stream of cars passing through Frederick headed for the assembly grounds, and from every direction it was the same. A large number of estimates placed the attendance at between 15 and 20 thousand.

It is very evident that the K.K.K. intend to thoroughly organize South Dakota. There are now members in almost every town and more joining all the time.

Nine miles from Aberdeen a funeral was conducted at Bath, South Dakota which utilized K.K.K. burial rites. It was the first time. The rites on that Wednesday afternoon in November, 1924 were for Matthew Chalcraft. Professor Thomas from Aberdeen conducted the liturgy at the church. At graveside the klan members in full regalia of robes and masks were present and carried out the ritual for the first time.

The *Aberdeen Evening News* of August 8, 1924, carried the news of the death of prominent citizen Isaac Daniel Tower. The former representative in the state legislature and the man who had secured the passage of the bill creating the Northern Normal and Industrial school in Aberdeen (now Northern State University) was killed in an accident in Harlowton, Montana. Funeral services occurred at the M.E. Church officiated by Reverend A.C. Canole. At the grave appeared eleven members of the Ku Klux Klan, clothed in full regalia, who offered up a prayer and deposited a wreath on the casket. Many wondered. Was this a kind act of generosity on the part of the Klan, or was there some connection between I.D. Tower and the Klan?

An October 27, 1921 editorial opinion in the *Brookings Register* signaled a sharply skeptical view of the growing Klan in South Dakota. "In case the Ku Klux Klan really wished to do a constructive act, we would recommend that the imperial wizard send a detail overseas to spirit Grover Cleveland Bergdoll back to this side and do some of their 'Americanization' work on him." (Note: Grover Cleveland Bergdoll was a draft dodger during World War I and escaped to Germany.)

The movie *The Birth of a Nation* played at the Brookings State Theater in September 1922. Touted as a production never equaled, it featured the biggest battle of the Civil War, Sherman's March to the Sea, Lincoln's assassination and a most favorable presentation of the Ku Klux Klan.

The *Brookings Register* publicized the movie's showing for September 25, 26 and 27. Twelve reels later and music by a live five-piece orchestra entranced the audience and solidified the view of the Klan as saver of America. New York showings cost $5 per seat (equivalent to $75 in 2023).

On August 27, 1923, two flaming crosses were seen in Montrose—one east of town, the other west of town—suggesting the Klan had arrived. However, the citizens were unsure if it was in fact the Klan or some individuals trying to create a little excitement.[49]

On February 20, 1924, Watertown residents watched a fiery cross burn just south of the city. Some 150 men took part in the ceremony, which was a signal that a local organization had been completed.[50]

Near the historic Strand Opera House in Ipswitch, a nearly twenty-foot-high fiery cross was seen burning right after politician Royal C. Johnson finished his stump speech. Because a large crowd was expected to gather, the culprits took advantage of the event to make a point. The congressman's speech had nothing to do with the subject of the Klan.[51]

The *Fiery Cross*'s May 28, 1924 issue reported

Iroquois, S.D.,—Thanks to the state office, Iroquois secured the services of a National speaker, who delivered an address before about 250 interested citizens and Klansmen....The speaker, during his two hour talk, explained very fully the aims and need for the organization in every community, handling his subject in an able manner; or as we might say, he was a big man with a Big Message, and he put it across.
***

IROQUOIS IN TAKES LARGE CLASS
Following the Invitational Meeting Iroquios Klan Takes in the Largest Class Yet Had

Birth of a Nation movie
promotion poster.
Public domain.

Iroquois, S.D.,—Iroquois is proud of its large class, the largest in the history of the klan, here, that was taken in last week following our invitational meeting, and if the way the requests for membership and information are being received are any indication, the next class will be still larger. We have the habit, and it will be a matter of a short time before it will be necessary to encroach on some one else's for material. Let the good work go on.[52]

The Big Stone Headlight newspaper from Big Stone City, South Dakota, reported on June 19, 1924,

The Iroquios KKK gathering in Lyman's pasture where the Klan initiated a class of new members. 65 cars parked while the ceremonies went on. Car lights went on as the dark descended, followed by the lighting of three giant crosses. About 11 o'clock the Klansman disbanded, entered their cars and quietly exited the pasture.

Other South Dakota towns/communities showing active KKK growth included Highmore, which "took in a good sized class recently and they are ready to take in another in a very short time,"[53] and De Smet, where a burning cross on the A.N. Waters farm at the north end of Second Street was seen. Later in August, a large ceremonial event was staged on a hillside two miles from the city. Two hundred Klansmen gathered and celebrated a cross and three Ks burning covered by a searchlight for the benefit of the crowd. At Bancroft, twenty miles from De Smet on the Arden Jenks farm, a cross was seen blazing in the night sky.[54]

Opposition to the Klan erupted in Woonsocket, Wagner and Redfield, whereas the Klan flourished in Stickney and Mt. Vernon. The *Mitchell Evening Republican* stated on May 6, 1924:

No Room for Klan

Woonsocket News: Organizers for the Ku Klux Klan are reported to be headed for South Dakota to complete an organization here. They have been working in Iowa and have that state organized.

And no doubt, the question will be put to many of our good citizens in the very near future, and it is going to be up to us citizens to answer the question. "Do we need a Ku Klux Klan organization in Woonsocket and vicinity?"

We understand the membership carries with it a payment of a fee, a portion of which goes to the organizer, and of course he will work hard for membership as it will be to his own financial interest to do so. The News is of the opinion that we have no room for a Ku Klux Klan here. We can settle our differences, if we have any, to the greater idea of harmony and good to the city and citizens. There shoulders be no need for any of us to hide behind the white robe. Let's stay out in the open and handle our affairs of life in the truest style of American sportsmanship. Let's be out and above board in all our dealings to mankind.

In Redfield, South Dakota, Mayor William Issenhuth stated "that he could see no reason for such an organization here although in some sections of the south land it is doing a great service."

In Wagner, South Dakota, the Klan accused local law enforcement of wasting their time. Instead of enforcing the law, the sheriff and deputies were going about collecting the names of local Klan members. The *Fiery Cross* reported in 1924:

Mt. Vernon Klansmen Believe in the Protection of the American Flag

Mt. Vernon, S.D.,—The Ku Klux Klan seems to be very active in and around Mt. Vernon as the men that have red American blood flowing through their veins and that love America more than any other country and they feel as though American needs their help as though they feel as though they have been protected by the American Flag and if the American Flag has protected them all of their lives, so now they see that America is endangered they are going to take their stand along besides the Klucker Man and protect the Flag Old Glory in all her splendor, and they have began to learn that the real men of America are joining all over the state and on the outside are this class of People: The Catholics, who has sworn his allegiance to a Foreign Power, the Jew who does not believe in the bible; the Negro who is black and is not eligible; the Woman Chaser; the Dope Peddler; and the people who are in the White Slave Market.

The *Dakota Kourier*, a Klan newspaper based in Spenser, South Dakota, noted:

Stickney, S.D.,—Last Friday night a cross was burned on the streets of Stickney and the scoffers now know that the Stickney Klan is a live bunch.... One recent Sunday morning four robed Klansmen attended the E.U.B. Church, walking up to the front and quietly taking seats remaining through the services.... The Klan is no longer looked upon as it was when it was first organized here, but the good people of Stickney are all glad of the fact that the Klan is here and here to stay.

9

BOOTLEGGING AND THE KKK IN THE RUSHMORE STATE

Y ou're under arrest!" shouted suspicious strangers as they raced to the haystack. It happened in Hutchinson County, where Leona Pietz's mother, father and hired hand were loading moonshine into a wagon for transport. The agents fired shots into the cornfield, but two—mother Emelia and the hired man—were able to get away. Adolph Schelske of Parkston was not as lucky. Federal agents swarming in quickly captured and arrested him.

According to Leona V. Pietz in her *Memories of a Bootlegger's Daughter*, it had been a family affair—father, mother, daughter. Bootlegging. Leona Pietz's father, Adolph, first started using a stovetop kettle to make a small amount of liquor for family and neighborhood gatherings about 1920. Gradually, he made more and more. Adolph, Emelia and Leona's whiskey was the best, even though many immigrants in that German Russian community stirred up and distilled their own alcoholic brew.

Prohibition implemented by the Eighteenth Amendment went into effect in 1920 and continued until 1933 when abrogated by the Twenty-First Amendment. The Ku Klux Klan seized on this new law, making alcohol manufacturing illegal, one of their causes for existence. Thus, Prohibition helped paved the way for the KKK resurgence in the 1920s. If the law could not deal with moonshiners, bootleggers and speakeasies, then the KKK would step in. The Klan went a step further, convincing Prohibition supporters that they—the Klan—could pick up the slack left by overworked police who were struggling to stop bootleggers and deal with crime in the area. And beyond that, the KKK would critique and expose lawmen who were not doing their jobs.

One example of a wayward lawman was Verne Miller. A personable, handsome, ambitious man from White Lake, South Dakota, his career began as an exemplary citizen serving in France with the 164th Infantry. Wounded twice, Verne received the French Croix de Guerre for bravery. Mustered out, he settled in Huron and joined the Huron city police force. He was dedicated and zealous, even to the point of arresting prominent Huron leaders.

Once when a mob appeared after a fight at the local theater, Miller arrived, drew his pistol, confronted the rowdies and then dispersed the angry crowd. A rift, however, soon appeared between Miller and Police Chief Johnson. By this time, Miller had thrown his hat in the ring for sheriff of Beadle County. Elected—narrowly—he became an active civic community leader. He volunteered as a founder of the Huron American Legion post and served as its delegate to the state legion convention. When Miller was running for

Proud law enforcement personnel in Brookings County display the results of several raids in the county that included confiscation of several firearms displayed at the corners of the table. *Courtesy of Chuck Cecil.*

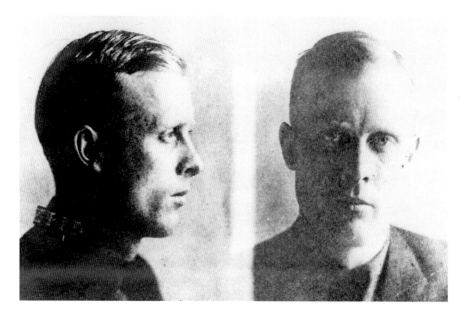

FBI photo of Verne Miller—war hero, sheriff, gangster. *Missouri State Archives.*

office, the *Evening Huronite* promoted his candidacy, editorializing that if he were elected, "crooks and licentious characters will have no protection, and the safety of our wives and children and the future well-being of our families will be fully guaranteed."

True to form, records show that Sheriff Miller located and destroyed nine moonshine stills during his first months in office. "So much bootlegged liquor was confiscated that Sheriff Miller began using it as antifreeze in the radiators of the sheriff department vehicles." Fearless, Miller was quick to draw his weapon, even firing on tourists for breaking basic traffic laws. A prison escapee hid in a pasture and, on hearing an automobile nearby backfire, thought Sheriff Miller was after him. He gave up.

Then trouble. Sheriff Verne Miller disappeared after withdrawing $4,000 from banks that had been garnered from property county tax collections. He was caught. After a brief stay in the Beadle County jail—now jailee and not jailer—he was sentenced to two years in the South Dakota State Penitentiary in Sioux Falls on April 4, 1923.

Once out, Miller's life went to the dark side. He got arrested for bootlegging. Fined and out of jail, he disappeared. In February 1928, ex-sheriff Verne was involved in a shootout at a Minneapolis speakeasy. With the infamous Barker gang, he robbed the Third Northwestern Bank in Minneapolis.

Tommy guns blazing, the gang mowed down two officers. The worst yet was Miller's involvement in the tragic Kansas City Massacre on June 17, 1933.

On November 29, 1933, Verne Miller's body was found in the outskirts of Detroit. When family and friends back in Huron heard of his death, they harbored mixed feelings. They would much rather remember the good, fearless sheriff and patriot than a rogue sheriff gone bad.[55]

The Ku Klux Klan often chided law enforcement for being too weak, too late or too corrupt. Sheriff Miller's behavior was an extreme example of law enforcement gone bad. There were times law enforcement looked the other way or simply winked at the latest report of criminal activity. In most cases, law enforcement could hardly keep up with the profusion of stills sprouting everywhere.

The Klan felt immigrants such as the German-Russian community in Hutchinson County and anyone not of WASP (White, Anglo-Saxon Protestant) heritage were the cause of America's problems. Immigrants from Europe were importing their cultures and their drinking habits, which contributed to more relaxed social mores.

This saw the emergence of the Woman's Christian Temperance Union and the Anti-Saloon League. Before long, the Klan reasoned, America would be overrun by Catholic foreigners contributing to societal decay. Bootleggers couldn't be arrested fast enough.

For the Pietz family at Parkston, economic challenges motivated Adolph Schelski to crank up the stills and become a moonshiner (manufacturer) and bootlegger (distributor). Daughter Leona Pietz described in her memoirs:

> *Drought, dust storms, grasshoppers and bank closings were the main causes of hard times. When the drought hit, lakes and rivers dried up, the livestock on the farms was starving. Crops weren't growing and the pastures had no grass.*
>
> *My father Adolph...and my mother Emelia, Ed* [the hired man], *and I being seven years old were all involved in the process....We all worked as a team because (our) farm was on the verge of failure in a horrible and environmental crisis, and there was a market for the (whiskey) in our German-Russian community.*

Leona Pietz helped maintain underground hiding spots; mix the oats, yeast and sugar; stir the mixture while it was fermenting; drain the liquid into the still; and discard the mash—often working into the wee hours of the morning.[56]

In November 1923, the residents of Plankinton, South Dakota, sighted a burning cross just north of the city.

The *Mellette County Pioneer* newspaper carried this story:

> *Plankington.—The residents of Plankington are at a loss to know whether or not there has been a chapter of the Ku Klux Klan organized in this community. The usual sign of their existence was manifested here by the burning of a large cross just north of the city. The sign is given credence by many, but it is also thought by some to be a prank of some of the boys about town.*

The presence and purpose of the Klan was made clear in a 1924 edition of the *Fiery Cross*:

> *PLANKINGTON CITIZENS HAVE THE VISION*
> *Plankington Klan Is Going After the Bootlegger in That Section*
>
> *Plankington, S. Dak.,—Plankington is doing their bit for the Klan movement. They sure have the vision. There was a large of number of men that sat and listened to a State Speaker explain the principles of the Ku Klux Klan and after listening to the Speaker for a short time they all seemed to think that the Organization was all O.K. as the meeting was almost 100%, even though there were a few bootleggers that seemed to be very much interested in the meeting also, and we want to say that they will have an Opportunity in the near future of getting acquainted with the Klan because we are going to give the officers of the law some Information that will lead to the arrest of some of the Violators of the Law and Justice in and around Plankington.*

On March 13, 1924, the *Miller Press* reported burning crosses in the South Dakota capitol of Pierre. Later in 1924, the *Fiery Cross* carried this story:

> *PIERRE KLAN WAKING THEM UP*
> *Pierre Klan Going Strong and each Meeting Brings More Citizens into the Empire*
>
> *Pierre, S.D.,—Usually this city puts on its sleeping garments about the middle of March of every odd year and keeps them on, with an occasional burst of wakefulness between sessions of the legislature, but this year it has*

been quite different. The cause being the organization of the Knights of the Ku Klux Klan in this city. Of course you see nothing of it in the daily papers. How could you expect to do that?

The Pierre Klan has been meeting regularly and not only meeting but taking in members.

It would be safe to say that within a few weeks the majority of the White, Protestant and Gentile Americans of the city will be affiliated with the movement, if the way they have been calling for information and joining up the past few weeks has any bearing on the subject.

On December 8, 1924, the *Mitchell Evening Republic* noted Articles of Incorporation had been filed in Pierre with Secretary of State C.E. Coyne by an organization known as the Women of the Ku Klux Klan. The doctrines were set forth, and a charter asked for organization in the state.

As the Ku Klux Klan proliferated, so did moonshining in South Dakota. State agents recorded in their annual report for 1923–24 178 arrests of "still" operators. (This does not count federal and local busts in the state.)

Author Chuck Cecil in his *Searching for the White Mule* illustrated numerous examples of typical sites and hiding places:

Stills steamed away in caves, isolated shacks, cornfields, timber stands, sandy river islands and on isolated farms. Stashes of booze were found in post holes, automobile spare tires, souped-up cars, straw stacks, potato piles, seeder boxes and even hallow cemetery grave markers…and weedy road culverts.…In Brookings County the road grader operator discovered more than a dozen one gallon jugs of booze buried up to their corked necks among roadside weeds near Bruce. Opposite each buried bottle, a piece of white cloth was tied to the fence as a subtle marker.

A Sisseton farmer manufactured and sold his powerful homemade "medication" at a rheumatism clinic he founded.…At the Hamandberg farm north of Harrisburg agents found a trap door under a resting cow in a barn stall leading to an underground still.…Near Elk Point in late 1924, agents found a 10-by-40 foot cave in a cornfield covered with boards and dirt. The dugout held a 100 gallon capacity still to process 40 awaiting barrels of fermenting mash. Agents also found a six burner stove, supplies of sugar, rye and yeast and an inside water well.…At the Schwenk farm in Yankton County on December 7, 1921, two trucks hauled away a plethora of beer making gear…booze trucked into Sioux Falls from the Al Capone gang in Minneapolis and multiple others.[57]

During 1924, one suspected bootlegger in Redfield, South Dakota, received Ku Klux Klan attention. Blacky Smith, a coal hauler by profession, was bootlegging on the side and was supposed to have a rather loose deal going at home where his wife was the principal attraction, or so the Klan believed.

The Klan contacted Blacky and suggested that he either leave town or the bullwhip and tar-and-feather medicine would be applied. Blacky and his wife left quickly for some unknown destination.[58]

The Klan continued to spread. The *Fiery Cross* carried this article in 1924:

OPEN MEETING AT CHAMBERLAIN
Open Meeting This City Proves There Are Many 100% Americans

Chamberlain S. Dak.,—On June 3rd, there was a large meeting held here to explain the principles of the Ku Klux Klan and after hearing the principles of the Klan explained everyone there affiliated with the Klan, and they were given the oath that night. After receiving the oath they all said that it was one of the Greatest oaths that they ever took and everyone said that it was Absolutely Christian 100% American and they said they would have every one that was eligible for the Movement in the Klan in a very short time. The boys at Chamberlain are real workers and they are going to lead every Community in South Dakota for Members.

Klan growth and activities continued in Blunt, South Dakota, with a banquet hosted by the Klan women and Murdo, South Dakota, taking in a large class in 1924.

Leona Pietz related in her memoir that when her father, Adolph, was arrested, he was fined one hundred dollars, which was a lot of money in those days, but he managed to scrape it together and avoid jail.

Ultimately, the family made a connection with two Sioux City, Iowa wife-and-husband bootleggers who sold her father "one hundred percent pure alcohol" and had it delivered to the farm. The family would all work to dilute the liquor with water and caramelized sugar to resell under their own label. Thus, the family worked primarily as bootleggers, rather than moonshiners, for the remained of Prohibition.

At another farm in Hutchinson County, officials got wind of a distillery and promptly arrested three moonshiners. "L.T. Kleinsasser, W.T. Warne and Peter Hofer confessed to the violation while giving up one stove and feed cooker, two sacks of bottles, 300 gallons of mash, one sack of rye, one cooler coil, six barrels, one milk can, one bushel basket and more. Firearms, knives and brass knuckles were also seized."[59]

Sometime later, even though the Schelske family no longer brewed their own whiskey, federal agents showed up to search the site. They found no distillery. But they did find a lone bottle of whiskey in the basement of the barn. Adolph was arrested a second time and sentenced to thirty days in the Hutchinson County jail. Leona Pietz remembered that the family stopped all moonshining and bootlegging activity at that time.[60]

10

THE KKK IN THE BLACK HILLS

Professor Charles Rambow of Rapid City, retired teacher at Sturgis High School and Black Hills University, is one of the foremost experts on the Ku Klux Klan in South Dakota. His story began with an epiphany: One day in 1970, his mother, living in Sturgis, cleaned out Charles's grandparents' closet and gave him what he thought was a choir robe that could be used for rags. The wrinkled rags, a robe, was actually his grandfather's Ku Klux Klan initiation robe.

Rambow's grandfather Hugh Caton, a judge in Meade County, was a member of the Ku Klux Klan. Charles was stunned. On further inquiry, he learned that both grandparents were members of the KKK back in 1921. Rambow's grandfather Judge Hugh Caton belonged to the Key City Klan in Sturgis. Rambow realized his grandfather, with their Anglican Irish heritage, disliked Catholics. Anti-Catholicism burned hot in the belly of the Klan. Its hatred joined traditional prejudices—anti-Black, anti-Jew, anti-Asian, pro-Nativism.

Charles Rambow suddenly had a topic for his master's thesis. His research began. He interviewed people who were members of the Black Hills Klans. He interviewed people who had family who were members or who had been targeted by the Klan. Rambow said the more interviews he did, the more people he found who remembered the Klan or had some sort of connection. His research kept growing. He learned nearly every community in the Black Hills had a Klan organization. In Spearfish, it was the Queen City Klan. In Lead-Deadwood, it was the Mile High Klan, in Rapid City the Gate City Klan.

Along with his research, he began to collect KKK artifacts, one of which includes a large KKK charter. He acquired the charter from Mrs. David Treber a retired fourth grade teacher. Husband David Treber was an electrician. One day, David Treber, while tearing out a wall in a house in Deadwood, came upon a large cavity, six by eight by eight feet, in the structure. In the hollowed-out space, he found a trove of KKK materials. Rolled up in the find was the well-preserved KKK charter.

On November 2, 1924, the Sturgis Key City Klan met secretly in the empty loft of a large barn east one block off Junction Avenue; 186 Klan members, 64 initiates and 20 bystanders gathered.

Charles Rambow displays his grandfather's Ku Klux Klan robe. *Courtesy of Charles Rambow Collection.*

A twelve-year-old girl was playing with her dolls downstairs. Curious, she climbed up the ladder to see what was going on. A Klan member caught her and threatened, "If you tell anyone and I ever find you, I'll cut off your ears."[61]

The *Fiery Cross* observed in a May 28, 1924 article:

> *Black Hills Getting the Best*
> *Better citizens of the Hills country are joining with this great organization.*
>
> *Sturgis, S.D.,—The Sturgis Klan is coming to the front fast. Already, with the work of the organization a few weeks old, there are a large number of Klansmen here and more to follow. Last Tuesday night, at 9:15, four fiery crosses blazed forth at the same time. Some lay it to the soldiers that are stationed here. The better class of people from this territory are coming forward and declaring themselves in favor of this great movement and for the high ideals taught by the Ku Klux Klan.*

The Black Hills Klan crept into the entire area by first infiltrating Sturgis, Deadwood and Lead. The Klan painted an image of itself as purely a social

Above: Sturgis Klan Initiation ritual on November 2, 1924. *Courtesy of Charles Rambow Collection.*

Opposite, top left: Charles Rambow robe showing Ku Klux Klan with "The drop of blood" insignia. *Courtesy of Charles Rambow Collection.*

Opposite, top right: Charles Rambow displays grandfather's Ku Klux Klan hood. *Courtesy of Charles Rambow Collection.*

organization. It held dances and promoted picnics, ladies' sewing circles and patriotic parades. At the same time, the Klan harbored simmering hatred at the presence of the Black soldiers stationed at Fort Meade. Trumping up animosity and mistrust, they stoked fear of immigrants and especially the Catholics. The KKK spread the false fear the pope was plotting to take over the country. Several times, KKK activists marched at the St. Martin's Academy, threatening the private Catholic school in the Black Hills. Students were trained to hide under their desks in case of rocks being thrown through the windows. The KKK also looked askance at the immigrant Chinese laborers who worked in the mines. During this time, when horse thievery and cattle rustling rattled the locals and the Klan felt that law enforcement dilly-dallied, they, the Klan, would take charge.

Nick Russell, in his book *Highway History and Back Road Mystery II*, related how:

> *In 1924, lawmen tracked down a gang of rustlers near Sturgis and wounded one in a brief gunfight before capturing them. The closest medical facility was at Fort Meade, and the wounded rustler was brought to the*

Author interviews Charles Rambow in Rapid City, South Dakota. *Author's collection.*

post's infirmary for treatment of his wounds. The local Klavern leader demanded that the rustler be turned over to the Klan for punishment. The post commander refused. The Klan's response was to threaten to march on Fort Meade and seize the wounded outlaw. They did not realize that they were now dealing with the United States Army, not a group of Catholic nuns or schoolchildren, or a lone soldier. Fort Meade's commanding officer

Lead, South Dakota, "Mile Hi" klavern charter. *Courtesy of Charles Rambow Collection.*

posted every available soldier on the Fort's perimeter, all heavily armed. One look at all of those determined troops, many of whom had been victims of Klan harassment in the past, was enough to convince them to slink away like the cowards they were. Relations between the Ku Klux Klan and the soldiers from Fort Meade continued to deteriorate, coming to a head in 1925. On the night of a community dance in Sturgis, the Klansmen erected three crosses on a hill between town and post, wrapped them in kerosene-soaked gunnysacks, and prepared to set them on fire as a warning to any soldiers or Catholics who planned to attend. But this time, their plans to send their message of hate and intimidation didn't work out. Several soldiers from Fort Meade decided that it was time to send a message of their own. They "liberated" two .30 caliber Browning water-cooled machine guns from the fort's armory and set them up on a hill across from the Klan gathering. As the hooded thugs started their crosses, the soldiers sent several long bursts of machine gun fire over their heads.

The Klans scrambled for cover behind trees and boulders and fired a few rounds back from handguns, which were no match for the soldier's automatic weapons....Local Klansmen realized that threats and intimidation go only so far...Klan activity came to a sudden halt in the Black Hills.

The *Fiery Cross* noted in its May 28, 1924 issue:

BLACK HILLS HAS MANY KLANSMEN
Report Has It That There Are Over Ten Thousand Klansmen in the Black Hills Country

Rapid City, S.D.,—It is reported that the soldier boys from Texas and other states, now stationed at Ft. Mead, held their first meeting and burned four large Fiery Crosses. While the crosses were burning the fire department turned out in an endeavor to quench the flames. However they were unsuccessful as they did not have water force sufficient to reach the top of the mountain on which each of the crosses were situated, and the Cross of Calvery [sic] was allowed to burn to the ground and to victory. Report also has it that there are between six and ten thousand Klansmen in the Black Hills country at the present time. With Klansmen among the soldiers stationed here, and the large class taken in the various cities of the district every week of late, it will be a short time before the Ku Klux Klan in the Hills territory will be the strongest institution in the state.

There was pushback in Deadwood, however, against the Klan despite its rapid growth and expanding influence. In the mid-1920s the Deadwood Fire Department published a notice saying, "If you are a Deadwood Fireman, we won't just kick you out, we're going to scratch your name right out of the records because you're a terrible American."

As the Klan grew, unsettling stories of actual violence continued to appear. One story Kenneth Stewart recalled in his 1973 Dakota Conference presentation "The Ku Klux Klan in South Dakota":

A former member of Klavern N. 48405 told me:

"I joined the Klan in Rapid City in the summer of 1924 and was a member until we disbanded in 1928. There was a woman here in Rapid City; a Mrs. Stoner, I believe. She was running a rooming house which had a nite-time sideline catering to local gents. This Mrs. Stoner was asked by a committee of the Klan to pack her bags and get out of town

Typical .30-caliber water-cooled machine gun at Fort Meade used to thwart Ku Klux Klan revelers. *World War I U.S. Army Signal Corps Collection, National Archives and Records Administration.*

in 24 hours. She told the committee where to go and what they could do when they got there. One member of the committee was a minister from a local church. When the Grand Dragon heard about this, he called a special meeting of the klavern. A car was ordered and seven men went down to her house on St. Patrick Street and kidnapped her. She was taken to a house in nearby Farmingdale southeast of Rapid City. There—was ordered to kiss the bible and swear to all present that she would honor the Klan and leave town. She had been drinking and started cussing again. Tar and feathers applied to her naked body soon calmed her down. She was dumped off at her house the next morning and by that evening had left town. Nothing was done about this by the law in Rapid City." [The individual who related this story to Kenneth Stewart stated he was not involved himself.]

The Homestake Mine, the largest gold mine in the United States, open from 1876 until 2002, served as a recruitment center for the Ku Klux Klan. Those applying for jobs in the mine were required to disclose their race, religion and ethnicity. This discriminatory practice ended in South Dakota in the 1930s.

A ghost town today, Terraville, South Dakota, hosted an active Klavern. Terraville sat on top of the richest lode of gold in the Hills. It birthed the Homestead Mining Company and once boasted being the fifth-largest town in the Black Hills with 775 citizens. A tunnel was constructed to connect Terraville to Lead. Eventually, Terraville, replaced by the present Open Cut Pit of the Homestead Mine, disappeared. In its prime, however, the Terraville Klan exerted its influence.

The *Dakota Kourier* published this article in 1924:

Interesting Letter from Terraville Klansman
A Terraville Klansman Is Sounding a Timely Warning to Careless People Who Fail to Live Up to the Law

Terraville, S. Dak.,—In these days when it seems that so little respect is paid to the laws of the land; when violations of law is so easy and so frequent, it would be well to pause and get back to the old idea that the duty of honest citizenship is to honor and observe the laws of State and Nation. Let every citizen of the United States, read that article of Abraham Lincoln. Let every American, every lover of liberty swear by the blood of the Revolution never to violate in the least particular the laws of the country and if ever to tolerate their violation by others. As the patriots of '76 did to support.

During Prohibition, the Black Hills' ghostly mountains and quiet gulches birthed hundreds of moonshine stills. Moonshiners topped the Ku Klux Klan hit list. Often the KKK complained and criticized the local law enforcement officials while touting themselves as saviors of the law.

Newspapers in the area revealed many secrets with stories about stills and stash discoveries. In 1923, Meade County deputy sheriff Fred Westgate reported that illegal stills were so prevalent in West River country that "one can hardly put his foot down without stepping on one."

Federal agents climbed down a ladder into a cave near Rumford in Fall River County in 1931.

They squeezed through a wall opening, where they found a one-hundred-gallon still. Rumford is an unincorporated town southeast of Edgemont, South Dakota.

Moonshiner Bert Miller of Hill City, South Dakota, along with Adolph Schelske of Hutchinson County, received the distinction of being "master distillers" because they brewed only the best. This title was expressed by Carl West, the Minneapolis Prohibition Enforcement Department's chief chemist in 1924.

On May 28, 1924, the *Fiery Cross* claimed,

Belle Fourche Promises to Be One of the Strongest in That Part of the County.

Belle Fourche, S.D.,—This week will see the initiation of the second large class to be taken into the Invisible Empire, Knights of the Ku Klux Klan in this city within the past few weeks. The Klan movement here is comparatively new and we, the Klan members, intend to make it one of the strongest movements of any place in this part of the state. Many who, when the Klan first began to organize hereabouts, were against or luke warm on the subject, are changing their minds and coming under the wire in fine shape.

An article in the *Argus Leader* on July 2, 1925, reported,

The Tri-State round up, one of the largest round ups in the west, will conclude it's three-day program at Belle Fourche on July 4, and the same day the interstate Konklave of the Ku Klux Klan will begin. Klansmen from all over the country will participate, but particularly from the Dakotas, Nebraska, Iowa, Minnesota, Wyoming, Montana, Colorado, Illinois, Indiana, Ohio and Wisconsin.

The *Argus Leader* followed up with this July 7 article:

Thousands Watch Klansmen

The grounds were turned over to the Ku Klux Klan organization at the close of the round up program. The location was ideal for the purpose with the horseshoe bend of Belle Fourche river, the high bluffs south and east and the gradual incline west. The grandstand, bleachers and all available seats, and automobiles massed in hundreds on elevations, were full of spectators looking down on the grounds with burning crosses and white robed figures.

The parade was led by Klan officials from North and South Dakota in robes of their positions. White robed figures four abreast, horses carrying robed Klansmen and beautiful floats, followed. They carried the largest display ever attempted by fraternal or civic organizations in South Dakota. Floats of "little red schoolhouse," "Goddess of Liberty" and "home" were noted specially, drawing enthusiastic applause. From elevations, spectators described the parade as resembling a snowy white electric serpent over a half mile in length winding gracefully about, from the grounds to town, back to the grounds and around the lighted tract, torches lighted on arena posts ahead of its progress. Dr. F.O. Rutledge, representative of the Imperial Wizard, was the principle speaker and was listened to attentively with much applause. A large fireworks display closed the program. Good order prevailed throughout the roundup and Klan demonstration. There was no trouble of any kind. Officers state there was very little moonshine. Only one accident was reported on Spearfish road. Two cars collided, and four occupants were injured slightly. The cars were righted and ran in on their own power.

Several newspapers, such as the *Belle Fourche Bee*, the *Northwest Post* and the Klan papers, estimated the roundup and Klan Konklave at up to 32,000 participants, the largest crowd ever in the Midwest Realm of the Klan. The parade itself dazzled the crowd as 760 robed and hooded Klansmen marched, 93 on mounted, sheeted horses prancing smartly in cadence.

An equally large and impressive Klan gathering took place in June 1925, near Spearfish. The following astounding report came from the *Black Hills Weekly Journal* (Deadwood, South Dakota):

Ku Klux Klan marches by the Duhamel Building in downtown Rapid City. *Courtesy of David B. Miller Papers, L.D. Case Library, Spearfish.*

HUGE THRONG SEES KLAN CEREMONIES: 10,000 PEOPLE AT CENTENNIAL FLAT (Spearfish)

A crowd estimated at between nine and ten thousand people witnessed the ceremonies of the Ku Klux Klan at Centennial Flat near Spearfish Thursday night, according to a Klansman who passed through town on the way to Iowa to visit relatives. More than 2,350 cars were parked on the grounds, it was said. Eleven crosses were burned, the largest being 150 x 500 feet in dimensions and located on a side hill. The statement was made that 260 men and 89 women were initiated during the ceremonies. The fireworks display cost $1,960.00.

Other towns in West River that reported Klan activity included Fort Pierre, Hayes, Hot Springs, Philip, Carter, Witten and Stamford. When the invitation breezed about to the public, its exclusive sting became obvious: "All gentile, protestant, American born men and women are invited to attend."[62]

110

In Custer, South Dakota, the *Custer Weekly Chronicle* reported on September 24, 1921:

> *The fight against the Ku Klux Klan is growing more interesting and more widespread every day and the Klan is fighting back against it's enemies with vigor. Various papers in many parts of the country have undertaken "exposures" of the organization and it's methods and aims, and the Klan has started or says it will start libel suits against those publications that misrepresent it....Meanwhile the Klan continues to grow in numbers with extraordinary rapidity, now having more than half a million members, and being organized in every state in the Union.* [Note: Membership in the national Klan reached its zenith year in 1925 with over 6 million members and $5 million in assets and cash.][63]

An act of charity by the Klan at Custer was reported in the *Custer County Chronicle* on July 1 and also in the *Rapid City Daily Journal* on July 6, 1925:

> *A sympathizing friend who went to the McKinney home immediately after his death was discovered, came to this office and told us that within an hour after Mr. McKinney's death, a representative of the Ladies Klan called on Mrs. McKinney and presented her with a purse of $25 and told her to bring the children to town and have them properly clothed and they would pay the bill.*

11

GUTZON BORGLUM

MEMBER AND LEADER
IN THE KKK

Gutzon Borglum, celebrated for the ill-fated original massive sculptures at Stone Mountain, Georgia, and the *successful* Mount Rushmore Colossal in South Dakota, was a member of and leader in the Ku Klux Klan. Borglum helped found the first Klavern in the Black Hills in 1922. Borglum's journey, however, is more than the shadowy path of the KKK. Detours, roadblocks and dead ends did not detract from Borglum's genius, brilliance and ultimate path to an astounding success. While successful in his career, his unwavering commitment to the supremacy of the Anglo-Saxon race smudges his legacy.

On August 10, 1927, Gutzon Borglum was handed four jackhammer bits from President Calvin Coolidge. Coolidge, wearing his traditional New England suit and vest, cowboy boots and oversized cowboy hat, had just given this short speech on the platform before an eager, curious crowd:

We have come here to dedicate a cornerstone that was laid by the hand of the Almighty. On this towering wall of Rushmore, in the heart

Gutzon de la Mothe Borglum, American sculptor of Mount Rushmore. *Courtesy of the National Park Service.*

of the Black Hills, is to be inscribed a memorial which will represent some
of the outstanding events of American history by portraying with suitable
inscription the features of four of our Presidents, laid on by the hand of a
great artist in sculpture.[64]

Borglum dramatically climbed to the top of the mountain, where he was joined by Jesse Tucker and crew. Tucker had been selected by Gutzon Borglum to function as the superintendent of the Stone Mountain project and was now assigned at Mount Rushmore. Borglum strapped himself into the bosun's seat with drill bits and jackhammer in hand. Slowly, Tucker, turning the winch, lowered Borglum over the granite cliff to a spot where special marks had been painted on the rock. Gutzon steadied himself and jackhammered a hole, then a second, third and fourth. Four master holes marked the beginning of the future depiction of George Washington.

Fourteen years later, four colossal portraits carved into the granite would beckon millions of Americans and citizens of the world as well to gaze in worshipful silence at what would be referred to as the *Shrine of Democracy.*

Tucker quietly dropped Borglum back down on the platform. Borglum, confident and with flair, handed one of the bits to President Coolidge. He gave a second drill bit to Doane Robinson, the state historian and original visionary for the Mount Rushmore monument, and a third to promoter Senator Peter Norbeck. The fourth drill bit Borglum prized for himself.

"When the ceremony ended, Coolidge asked Gutzon how the mountain carving was going to be financed. He suggested that Gutzon visit him in Washington so they could discuss the matter and devise a way. The backers of Rushmore were delighted. The President's suggestion was exactly what they were hoping for when they invited him (Coolidge) to the Hills."[65]

Gutzon Borglum first came in contact with the KKK through an invitation to carve a monument on Stone Mountain near Atlanta, Georgia, to commemorate the glory of the Confederate soldiers. The invitation came from Helen C. Paine. Paine had lost her husband in the Civil War. As president of the Atlanta chapter of the United Daughters of the Confederacy (UDC), she wondered if a memorial could be carved on the face of Stone Mountain. Her inspiration for the invitation came from a compelling essay written by the editor of the *New York American,* John Temple Graves. Graves published in the *Atlanta Georgian* "that Stone Mountain might be an artist's grand canvas to celebrate the South's courageous battle for independence."[66]

Borglum, always fascinated by the big, bold and colossal, packed his imagination into his valise and hastened to Atlanta to assess the possibilities.

He had been chosen over some of the great sculptors of the day such as Lorado Taft and others.

By then, Sam Venable, owner of Stone Mountain and a member of the Ku Klux Klan, had agreed to donate the cliff for the monument. At a

Borglum in bosun chair inspecting sculpting work while dangling on the face of Mount Rushmore. *Courtesy of the National Park Service.*

dedication ceremony on Saturday, May 16, 1916, Venable turned the deed over to the Stone Mountain Memorial Association.

On December 17, 1915, just three weeks after Colonel Simmons burned that first crudely constructed cross up on Stone Mountain and four months after Gutzon's visit to Atlanta, Helen Paine wrote to Borglum:

> *"Birth of a Nation" will give us a percentage of Monday's matinee....I feel it is due to the Ku Klux Klan which saved us from Negro domination and carpetbag rule, that it be immortalized on Stone Mountain. Why not represent a small group of them in their nightly uniform approaching in the distance?*

Borglum, with dreams already swirling, did not know how to respond. The new KKK had not existed when he first went to Georgia. He needed time to assess the situation, but he did not want to risk offending Mrs. Paine and Sam Venable and lose their support. He revised his plans for the memorial and included a KKK altar in the scene.[67]

The Stone Mountain project needed money. Lots of it. Millions. The Memorial Association settled on the Ku Klux Klan, as it had mushroomed in wealth due to the incredible success of KKK fundraisers Edward Young Clarke and Elizabeth Tyler. All along, Borglum believed wealthy patrons would be eager to fund the project. He was sorely disappointed both at Stone Mountain and later at Mount Rushmore. Bursting with rage, he blistered the ears of anyone who would listen. "Shame on you. Your apathy and unpatriotic response is both disgusting and repugnant."

At first, the new Ku Klux Klan paraded as simply a civic, social fraternal order that stressed Protestant, 100 percent Americanism and the supremacy of the white race. During the First World War, the Klan pursued its goals of rooting out shirkers, idlers, alien enemies and any other who might threaten the war effort.[68]

Gradually, the Klan developed into an aggressive movement preaching 100 percent Americanism or Nativism. Nativism is the policy of protecting the interests of the native-born by opposing immigration, people of color, Jews, Catholics, Asians and all aliens. The Klansmen pictured themselves as self-appointed vigilantes and moralists. They fought dope, bootlegging, rustling, graft, violation of the Sabbath, prostitution, adultery, shady business deals/ethics or any scandalous behavior that appeared to be less than 100 percent American. Borglum as a Klansman cared little for robes, hoods/ masks and rituals. He prized and worked tirelessly for financial support for the monuments.

He also took an active role in every presidential campaign from 1904 on. He had direct access to seven presidents during his lifetime. According to Howard and Audrey Shaff in *Six Wars at a Time: The Life and Times of Gutzon Borglum*, he believed that a group like the KKK could help organize the rural states to promote the National Non-Partisan League, an agrarian reform movement. He thought it would take up the plight of farmers, building a national party.

John Gutzon de la Borglum was born on March 25, 1867, in Idaho territory, one of two sons of one of the wives of a Danish Mormon immigrant. He apprenticed in a machine shop, graduating from Creighton Preparatory School. His artistic talent blossomed during his stay doing commissions in London and Paris. In Paris, he excelled as a portrait painter of exceptional talent. Then, like his sculptor brother Solon Borglum, he flourished and excelled as a talented sculptor, having been tutored in the studio of Auguste Rodin.

His incredible talent and genius soared. A partial list of his sculptured works includes *Apache Pursued*; *The Boer Soldier* bronze statue; *Statue of Union General Philip Sheridan* in Washington, D.C.; a bust of *Abraham Lincoln* in the United States Capitol crypt in Washington, D.C.; *Ulysses S. Grant* heroic statue; the *Mares of Diomedes*; gargoyles for the class of 1879 dormitory at Princeton University; *Mask of the Angel of Annunciation*; *Conception*; *Saints and* Apostles for the Cathedral of St. John the Divine in 1901; *William Jennings Bryan* statue dedicated by Franklin Roosevelt; *Woodrow Wilson* statue located in Poznan, Poland; the *Aviator, John William Mckay* statue; *The Battle of Gettysburg*; *Rabonni*; *John Peter Altgeld Memorial* in 1915 in Chicago; *Thomas Paine* in Montsouris, France; and monuments and sculptures all around the world.

Borglum, a multitalented artist, expanded his gifts and passions into urban design and numerous variegated structures. He worked with a committee that planned New York City's Central Park. He designed plans for an opera house and a waterfront promenade for Corpus Christi, Texas. Borglum corresponded with Frank Lloyd Wright about architecture, modernism and the layout of factories. He designed public fountains, coins, buildings, airplanes and parts for airplanes, bridges and educational curricula. He often believed that his truth was the only truth and was disgusted when others did not see things his way.

He gave speeches on art and politics in America. Gutzon Borglum was indefatigable, a one-man industry.

In November 1922, Borglum met David C. Stephenson when they both attended a national Klonvocation. The two clicked. Stephenson and

Borglum discovered that their political beliefs were a match. Stephenson was exceedingly successful in recruiting almost a third of all the white, native-born Protestant men of Indiana (250,000) to the Ku Klux Klan. He was given the title King Kleagle and then Grand Dragon of the Indiana Klan.

Stephenson, as a showman and organizer par excellence, became one of the most powerful men in the state. He controlled the governor's election and that of several state legislators and hand-picked the candidate for mayor of Indianapolis.

Stephenson made friends easily and was pleasantly gregarious. Based on the commission scheme of the Ku Klux Klan led by Clarke and Tyler, he became very wealthy in a short time. He loved money. He also loved women, which eventually led to his downfall, arrest and prison. He and Gutzon Borglum had mutual goals: Stephenson the White House, Borglum a pathway for his political ambitions. Borglum passionately wanted to make a difference for the welfare of the nation; he championed the rural farmers. Together, Borglum and Stephenson became collaborators. Unabashed, Stephenson proclaimed:

> *God help the man who issues a proclamation of war against the Klan in Indiana now.... We are going to Klux Indiana as she has never been Kluxed before....I'll appeal to the ministers of Indiana to do the praying for the Ku Klux Klan and I'll do the scrapping for it....And the Fiery Cross is going to burn at every crossroads in Indiana, as long as there is a white man in the state.*[69]

However, cracks began to appear in the Klan organization. Scandal with fundraisers Clarke and Tyler ended in arrests. Then with the appearance of Hiram Wesley Evans, Evans and Stephenson, engineered a coup demoting Colonel Simmons. Evans became Imperial Wizard of the Ku Klux Klan. Stephenson was confirmed as head of the Indiana Klan and anointed Grand Dragon of the Northern Realm of twenty-two states.

Gutzon Borglum attended a prayer breakfast with Simmons, Evans and Stephenson and the other rebelling members on the morning of the convention coup. Immediately after the coup, Borglum was named Imperial Kloncilium. This promoted him to the executive board. Borglum was no longer an outsider, no foot soldier. For a brief time, Gutzon Borglum, the would-be sculptor of Mount Rushmore, became a high officer in the Ku Klux Klan.[70]

Borglum's friendship with Stephenson and the rift with Evans were enormously important at Stone Mountain. Gutzon tried to intervene in a squabble between Sam Venable and Nathan Forrest against Evans and his followers. Venable and Forrest were loyal to Colonel Simmons. Borglum realized he could not afford this unwanted publicity.

After Stephenson's dramatic investiture before thousands of robed Klansmen, Borglum, as a voracious reader and writer, began to express his deeper nastiness. Borlum appeared to be influenced by the likes of the French racial theorist Joseph Arthur de Gobineau. Gobineau was a French aristocrat who promoted legitimizing racism by using "scientific" theory and racial demography. Gobineau's writings later influenced the Nazis.

Borglum wrote to Stephenson:[71]

> *The Nordic races have been and continue today as the pioneers of the world. They are the builders of world empires…these venturesome peoples who have subdued savages, beautified and peopled what was in the Roman day the wilderness and is now the richest, most comfortable, best established, most sought portion…of the earth….America has been peopled by these free, independent thinking races….The dark races have never moved in block….The oriental has no constructive initiative….The Nordic has ever been a camper maker.*[72]

Borglum's racism philosophy exploded in this section to Stephenson:

> *Every step in the course of west world civilization has been opened up by Anglo-Saxon Americans.*
>
> *If you cross a thoroughbred with a jackass you get a mule. If you cross a purebred with a mongrel you get a mongrel. So in races…if you cross any of the others with each other it is curious that the lowest race in civilization is the strongest physically and breeding (crossed) is always down. A Negro and Jew will produce Negro, but Hindu and Jew = Jew. Chinese and Jew, offspring Jew. Italian and Jew, offspring Jew. Any European race and Jew, offspring Jew.*[73]

In further correspondence with Stephenson, it appears that Borglum suggested that "aliens" be treated as a lower class: "A certain portion of all aliens should have their labor designated for them until such time as the government could control it's trained and untrained labor market and move the surplus as needed."

Borglum further revealed his prejudices in the choice of language he used in another correspondence with Stephenson. By December 1923, he seemed to have grown disenchanted with the Ku Klux Klan and its failing political efforts: "A Jew, a negro, or a Romanist could not crawl into a more cowardly position nor seek neutral ground more quickly that did every Klan leader I appealed to."

D.C. Stephenson, a political rising star, had a dark side. When drunk, he beat or abused or abandoned his wives. Nettie White, he abandoned; Violet Carroll, he divorced; Martha Dickenson, he committed bigamy against by marrying Martha Sutton. In 1925, Stephenson, publicly a prohibitionist and a defender of "protestant womanhood," found himself a defendant in the most spectacular trial in Indiana history. He was accused of kidnapping a twenty-eight-year-old clerk, Madge Oberholtzer, and repeatedly raping her on an overnight train from Indianapolis to Chicago. When they reached the city, Oberholzer was checked into a hotel with him, and then, accompanied by a Stephenson bodyguard, she slipped out to buy a hat. She bought the hat and surreptitiously purchased some mercury bichloride powder, which she swallowed a month later. When she was dying, she claimed that she did this as a way of forcing Stephenson to take her back to Indiana. There was some doubt at the trial about whether Oberholtzer's death was caused by the poison or by infection from the deep bites that Stephenson supposedly inflicted all over her body.

David Curtis Stephenson was sent to prison on a conviction of murder in the second degree and was sentenced to serve thirty-three years to life imprisonment.

Stephenson remained close to Borglum until Borglum's death in 1941. He also remained close to Borglum's widow, Mary, by corresponding from prison. Gutzon and Mary Borglum always insisted that Stephenson had been framed for political reasons. Some evidence suggests this may be true, even though Stephenson was no saint.

Stephenson was discharged from prison in 1956.

By 1924, Gutzon Borglum had carved General Robert E. Lee's figure on Stone Mountain. Jefferson Davis and Stonewall Jackson's images remained. Borglum expected to get paid for his work. He wasn't.

Angered—trouble brewed. Eventually, Gutzon was fired by the Stone Mountain Association. It accused him of disloyalty, offensive egotism, delusions of grandeur and excessive concern for money and notoriety. Gutzon reacted—enraged. He destroyed the models of the bas reliefs and dropped them over the cliff.

The association, in turn, considered the destroyed models its property. Now, also enraged, the leadership went to the sheriff. Borglum was at Sam Venable's home when Jesse Tucker burst into the house and practically bodily forced Borglum out into his automobile. They barely got out of the driveway when the sheriff and a posse arrived with a warrant for Gutzon Borglum's arrest, charging him with "willful destruction of Association property." "The chase went on for several hours....At times Tucker ordered Gutzon to get down on the floor less [sic] there be shooting. Eventually, in the early morning hours they crossed the border safely in North Carolina. Gutzon was safe, but a fugitive from Georgia justice."[74]

In September of 1924, Borglum wired Doane Robinson to tell him, "I am ready to come to Rapid City!"

Gutzon Borglum ended his affiliation with the Klan in 1925. However, he continued to cling to his version of racism—superiority of the Aryan race and white supremacy—even while working on Mount Rushmore.

Borglum died on March 6, 1941, at seventy-three years of age. His son Lincoln finished the iconic massive rock sculpture at Mount Rushmore on October 31, 1941—fourteen years after its beginning in 1927.

12

THE KLAN FLOURISHES IN BORDER STATES AND TRISTATE REALM

Terror, intimidation and violence, though rare, did erupt not only in South Dakota with the murder of Father Belknap but also in border states. One egregious example took place in Duluth, Minnesota, on June 14, 1920. The John Robinson Circus arrived in town for a free parade and a one-night performance. Local African Americans were hired to assist as day labors in basic tasks as props men and cooks for workers and patrons. Two local teenagers, Irene Tusken, age nineteen, and James "Jimmie" Sullivan, eighteen, met at the circus and, after the show the next day, went behind the scenes to watch the Black workers dismantle the menagerie tent, load wagons and prepare the circus to move on. It is unclear what then actually happened between Irene Tusken, Jimmie Sullivan and the circus workers. Later, Sullivan told his father that he and Tusken were held up by three circus workers at gunpoint and robbed, and Irene was raped. Police were called in. The one hundred or so Black workers were rounded up. Elias Clayton, Issac McGhie and Elmer Jackson and three others were identified as the culprits. Two days later, Irene was taken to her local doctor; an examination gave no evidence that she had been assaulted or raped.

The six men were lodged in the Duluth local jail. Word spread. Soon an angry mob of five thousand citizens appeared, attacked the jail and dragged out Elias, Issac and Elmer. They conducted a kangaroo court and convicted them of the rape of Irene Tusken. The mob dragged the trio out to a light pole at the intersection and Second Avenue East, beat them, stripped them and lynched them.

Despite a lack of evidence, seven Black men were indicted for the crime of rape and served up to four years each.

Three white men—Louis Dondino, Carl Hammerberg and Gilbert Stephenson—part of the mob, were convicted of rioting, but no one has ever been charged for the murder of Elias, Issac and Elmer.

The *Chicago Evening Post* mused: "This is a crime of a Northern state, as black and ugly as any that has brought the South in disrepute. The Duluth authorities stand condemned in the eyes of the nation." Police officers who had been at the jail the night of the lynchings obviously failed to perform their duty. They continued to be employed as police officers in 1925 and 1926 and, by the way, were also members of the KKK.[75]

In the 1920s, the Klan began to spread, purporting to offer solutions to whatever a community's concern that needed to be addressed. Every county in Minnesota had a different worry. The worry could be that the Catholics were showing up more and more in their community; too many Germans were moving in; the Knights of Columbus were seen as an organization pledged to exterminate Protestantism; or that the Catholic churches were arsenals to be used to assassinate Protestants.

Intolerance, subtle and more lethal than the Black Plague, infected the anxious populace. The Klan's official newspaper *Call of the North* identified immigration as America's most pressing problem. All "outsiders" targeted included Catholics, German and Jewish immigrants and Blacks who relocated from the South. By 1923, Minnesota had spawned fifty-one chapters of the KKK with over 30,000 members. The Klan counted 100,000 members at Minnesota's zenith.

The first Klan parade in Minnesota took place in Albert Lea in 1923. Soon thereafter, the first state Klan Konklave took place in Faribualt in 1924. Owatonna, also in southern Minnesota, hosted several Konklaves highlighted by parades, ballgames and even weddings. A twenty-acre site in Owatonna served as a place for the 1926 State Konklave and is still known today as "Klan Park." Three couples exchanged vows at the 1925 state meeting at the Steele County Fairgrounds with a spectacular backdrop of a flaming cross.

Cross burnings took place in multiple communities such as Brainerd, Bass Lake and Red Wing, where startled residents witnessed lit-up skies. A Waseca Klavern was chartered in 1926, along with Klaverns in Kenyon, Dodge Center and Rochester. In Virginia, the Virginia School Board members all claimed to be Klan members, mainly to keep schools public in that Iron Range city, thereby discouraging the start-up of Catholic schools.

The mayor of St. James, while in office, served as the Grand Dragon for the Klan's Tri-state Realm.

St. James became the hub for common Klan activities in the three states of North and South Dakota and Minnesota.

Minnesota Klansmen were adamant supporters of Prohibition. Since there were many stills throughout Minnesota, the Klan zeroed in on Prohibition as part of its mission. In Waseca County, the *Waseca Herald* noted, "The moonshine game is hard to put down. Like swatting a fly. When you kill one of the darn things, it seems a dozen come to his funeral."[76]

Minnesota charities and churches were often the benefactors of Ku Klux Klan charity. Robed Klansmen would come into a church and give a financial gift. For example, a Methodist church in Paynsville received a gift for church repair. There was little or no distinction between membership in a local Klavern and membership in a Protestant church. Many Methodist, Presbyterian and Congregational ministers were not only members of the KKK but also speakers going about promoting the Klan and what it stood for.

Hawley, Minnesota, a Lutheran enclave, was an active site for Klan activity. A historian estimated that ministers of half of the Norwegian Lutheran Evangelical congregations in the area were members or tacit supporters of the Klan.

Carleton College, established by the Congregational Church in Northfield, Minnesota, was known as "Karleton College." Effigies of African Americans were often strung up during homecoming festivities, a tradition that continued at Carleton until the 1930s. Hooded and robed students made up the Karleton Kosmopolital Klub.[77]

The Ku Klux Klan in border state Nebraska began to recruit members in 1921. In late 1921, the Klan announced twenty-four locals had been organized. Eight hundred people a week were joining. By the summer of 1922, the *Monitor,* Omaha's leading Black newspaper, estimated Nebraska Klan membership at one thousand. According to the Klan headquarters, membership soon reached forty-five thousand. The Klan became active in Lincoln, Omaha, Fremont, York, Grand Island, Hastings, North Platte and Scottsbluff. In addition to these communities, its members sprouted like crabgrass around the state.

Even though there is no hard evidence that the Ku Klux Klan had any part in it, the Klan benefited from an egregious act similar to the Duluth lynchings. It happened in 1919 in Omaha, Nebraska, when William Brown, a Black packinghouse worker, allegedly assaulted nineteen-year-old Agnes

Lobeck and her nineteen-year-old companion Millard Hoffman. Brown was accused of stealing seventeen dollars while holding a gun on Hoffman and raping Agnes.

Millard Hoffman and a mob of nearly four to five thousand irate Omaha citizens quickly gathered. They surrounded the courthouse where Brown was jailed. They demanded immediate justice. The mayor, E.P. Smith, armed with a revolver, resisted and was overpowered and hanged from a trolley wire.

While the mayor survived and recovered, the incensed mob dragged Brown from the courthouse and into the street. They shot and lynched him. The out-of-control crowd then went on a rampage, looting and causing destruction throughout the city. Soldiers from Fort Crook and Fort Omaha arrived to restore order.

The Klan actually benefited from his horrendous incident. The crime gave evidence there was a race problem in Omaha and that the local officers were insufficient to retain law and order. The Klan gleefully touted itself as a needed law-and-order resource to be called on.[78]

In 1925, the Klan state convention in Lincoln coincided with the state fair. Conventioneers invited fair attendees to join an all-day Klan picnic. Crosses were burned. A parade with floats and 1,500 marchers moved along Lincoln streets. The picnic hosted 25,000 people. It featured a fireworks display and a Klan wedding, with the bride, groom and minister all wearing hoods and gowns.[79]

In 1925, Hiram Wesley Evans, the Imperial Wizard of the Klan, traveled through the state and made appearances in Omaha, Lincoln, York, Hastings, North Platte and Sidney. In Grand Island, boys joined the junior Klan and the girls Tri-K clubs. For women of the state, the Klan organized an auxiliary known as Women of the Klan.

Some Nebraskans joined the Klan believing it would oppose the doctrine of evolution, support law enforcement and limit the influence of the Catholic Church. Protestantism and patriotism were wed in the minds and doctrines of the KKK.

In Grand Island, Nebraska, seven Klansmen appeared at the First Christian Church, led the congregation singing "America" and left a $25 donation ($350 in 2024).

In Fairfeld, Nebraska, a minister of the First Christian Church, G.W. Adkins, announced he was a member of the Ku Klux Klan. He was joined by seventy-five robed Klansmen who sang "America," and all knelt to pray.

Many Protestant churches were concerned about declining morals and maintaining biblical orthodoxy. The Klan agreed. The government appeared to be less than successful in containing bootlegging.

The Klan, well represented in police departments, promised to aid law enforcement. Elmer E. Thomas, a federal agent in 1924, estimated there were two thousand bootleggers in Omaha alone.[80]

The relationship between the Klan and the church became a divisive issue. In Hastings, after a revivalist proclaimed the virtues of the KKK, the church mysteriously burned down. Some business leaders denounced the Klan as un-American; others openly admitted their association with it. In Lincoln, one clothing store advertised "K uppenheimer K orrect K lothes" to attract Klan business.[81]

The Nebraska Klan lingered into the 1930s but eventually faded almost entirely from view. Its primary appeal to fraternalism, racism, nativism, anti-Catholicism and 100 percent Americanism had not and has not entirely disappeared from the minds and souls of Nebraskan citizenry. Nebraska's Klan membership numbered about forty-five thousand members.

According to the *Sioux Falls Argus Leader*, Ku Klux Klans Tri-state Realm activities accelerated in each of the following years:

October 3, 1925 A Tri-state Konklave met one-half mile east of the county farm in Sioux Falls. The afternoon celebration featured band concerts, thrilling aeroplane stunts, jumping, and public lectures by speakers of national reputation, who would discuss topics of interest to all true Americans. The month before September 9th, a permit had been granted, provided the paraders would march unmasked. evening on the September date featured men and women's drill teams, band concerts, speakers, public initiation of men and women and fireworks.

August 28, 1926 A tri-state "konklave" gathered 5,000 participants for the public program slated for 9:30. Speeches and music followed. One speaker was J. A. Jeffries of Aberdeen, Imperial representative of the Klan in South Dakota. The women's drill team performed, followed by fireworks on the nearby hill.

August 15, 1927 Thousands gathered for the tri-state Konklave of the Ku Klux Klan at the Klan grounds east of Sioux Falls. The featured speaker was Dr. Hiram W. Evans, Imperial Wizard of the Ku Klux Klan coming from Atlanta, Georgia. The assembly began with a picnic lunch,

followed by sports. After Dr. Evans' address, a parade was assembled on
East Eighth street in the evening. Prizes were awarded for the best floats
that traveled in the down town business section.

Border state Montana caught the KKK fever. The Montana Klan originated in Harlowtown in 1921. It established headquarters in Livingstone by 1923. More than 5,100 Montanans joined the movement coming from forty-six Montana communities such as Missoula, Billings, Whitehall, Havre, Laurel, Livingston, Miles City and Helena. According to historian Christine Erickson, associate history professor at Indiana University–Purdue University Fort Wayne, "One city where the Klan wasn't welcome was Butte, home to a large number of immigrant miners, Irish Catholics and committed drinkers."

"Our men have orders to shoot any Ku Kluxer who appears in Butte," Sheriff Jack Duggan is said to have ordered. This was reported by Erickson in the spring edition of *Montana: The Magazine of Western History.* Still, nearly two hundred men joined the Klan chapter in Butte between 1923 and 1929.

Grand Dragon Lewis Terwillinger commenting on the aura of Butte, "We realize that Butte is the worst place in the state of Montana, so far as, alienism and Catholicism are concerned."

Several factors led to the demise of the Klan in Montana. One was that Grand Dragon Lewis Terillinger was a stickler for Klan rules. He is known to have kicked out some prominent members in Harlowtown for being alien—born in Canada. A second reason for decline was the expense to maintain membership with dues, taxes and the requirement to buy one's own robe and hood from headquarters in Atlanta. A third reason for decline was the intimidation, arson, cross burnings and other violent acts common in the South reflecting on their image in the West.

According to a 2021 email Christine Erickson wrote to this author, "Many Montana Klansmen traveled to Belle Fourche in the early 1920s to attend a big fair—they probably met some Klansmen from South Dakota as well. The Grand Dragon Lewis Terwillinger was pretty excited about it and hoped that Montana would be able to send a marching band. I don't think they did although apparently decked out horses participated."

Clearly the South Dakota border states essentially helped legitimize the Ku Klux Klan and foster its presence and activities in the Rushmore State during the early twenties and beyond.

13

REVEREND HALSEY AMBROSE

GRAND FORKS, NORTH DAKOTA

He arrived with glowing credentials and impeccable achievements. Reverend F. Halsey Ambrose had established himself as a spellbinding orator, an indomitable opponent of the Roman Catholic Church and an agitator for stricter enforcement of Prohibition—he was an easy choice. Neither his fundamentalism nor his championing of nativist sentiments was a problem for the members of the First Presbyterian Church in Grand Forks, North Dakota. Recommended, called and warmly embraced, Reverend Ambrose arrived to begin his pastoral duties on September 7, 1918.

A Presbyterian minister from Madison, Wisconsin, Reverend George E. Hunt, had prophesied to the Grand Forks church, "You will have a very vigorous preacher, an active pastor and citizen. I predict a successful ministry in your city for him."[82]

Halsey Ambrose claimed to have both a college and divinity degree when he provided pulpit supply at a small church in Carollton, Maryland, in 1908. Ambrose then moved to Footville, Wisconsin, where the Madison Presbytery enrolled him as a Presbyterian minister. From 1913 to 1918, he served at the First Presbyterian Church in Marshfield, Wisconsin, where he doubled the church membership and became active in Prohibition and patriotic activities.[83]

When the Ku Klux Klan came to Grand Forks, North Dakota, its modus operandi was to make a first contact with the leading Protestant minister in town. The Klan salesman would offer the minister free membership and the privilege of acting as a Kleagle, a local recruiter. Hundreds of ministers accepted the offer, becoming high-ranking officers in local Klaverns. Some even went on to become national Klan lecturers.[84]

The Klan recruiter to Grand Forks came from Indiana. The first minister the recruiter approached was F. Halsey Ambrose. He had learned of Ambrose's gifts and outstanding leadership at First Presbyterian Church. Ambrose's views paralleled the views of the Klan. In fact, Ambrose met the requirements for a Ku Klux Klan organizer admirably: fiery speaker, conservative, anti-Catholic, Prohibition champion.

For years, some 1,200 people of all denominations filled the Presbyterian sanctuary for his Sunday night services. No other Protestant minister in town approached this attendance record. Halsey advertised the evening's topic on the bottom edge of the Saturday evening and Sunday morning editions of the *Grand Forks Herald*. He ridiculed modernism in religious thought and the teaching of evolution or "fool science."[85]

Quickly, Reverend Ambrose became the darling of the Ku Klux Klan. On June 4, 1922, Grand Forks No. 1 was officially awarded a Klan charter. The Grand Forks Klan, numbering several hundreds of people received the name the "Ansax Club," while leader Ambrose was awarded the title the "Exalted Cyclops."

Through his efforts, two faculty members of the University of North Dakota in Grand Forks were fired. They had supported the work of the Nonpartisan League, which Ambrose labeled "Socialist" and "Bolshevist."[86]

The Nonpartisan League, founded by Arthur Townley in 1915, advocated on behalf of small farmers and merchants in North Dakota. It urged state control of mills, grain elevators, banks and other farm-related industries. It intended to reduce the power of corporate and political interests in Minneapolis and Chicago. Arthur Townley, a flax farmer from Beach, North Dakota, along with a friend, Frank B. Wood, drafted a radical political platform in order to address many of the concerns of the farmers.

In 1915, small farmers in North Dakota saw themselves exploited by out-of-state companies. Townley hit the road. Farmers signed up by the hundreds, each making a payment of six-dollar dues. In the 1918 state election, the Nonpartisan League won full control of both houses of the state legislature. It proceeded to establish state-run agricultural enterprises as the North Dakota Mill and Elevator, the Bank of North Dakota and a state-owned railroad. The legislature established a statewide graduated income tax, authorized a state hail insurance fund and developed a workmen's compensation fund that assessed employers. In order to aid citizens in financing and building homes, the Nonpartisan League set up a Home Building Association.

Reverend F. Halsey Ambrose, charismatic preacher/leader who promoted Ku Klux Klan beliefs and activities in the Grand Forks, North Dakota area. Sketch from paper, "The Ku Klux Klan in Grand Forks, North Dakota" by William Harwood. *Courtesy of the South Dakota Historical Society, Pierre, South Dakota.*

In 1919, Reverend Ambrose, assisted by the *Grand Forks Herald,* blasted the Nonpartisan League by publishing a pamphlet titled "A Sermon on Applied Socialism." It sold over five thousand copies in fourteen days. Socialism and Bolshevism were no idle terms in Ambrose's view.

Ambrose was unabashed in denouncing Roman Catholics and their papism from the pulpit. The unfounded fear fostered by the Klan and promulgated by Ambrose was that the Catholics would dominate the town spiritually and politically. The Klan cheered with glee. The Catholics must be halted.

The Klan continued to grow in Grand Forks mostly because they had this charismatic leader in F. Halsey Ambrose. The Sunday evening services provided a megaphone for gullible businessmen to believe that Catholics presented a threat to their livelihoods. In sermons and lectures, in addition to the Catholic threat, Ambrose thrived as an ardent proponent of moralism, Prohibition and law and order. He opposed immigrants, divorce, motion pictures, free expression of sexuality and the rapidity of change. His influence spread.

In a testimony Ambrose gave at the state capitol in Bismarck in 1923, defending the Klan, he implied that the hundreds of Klansmen in Grand Forks and around the state were pillars of the community. He maintained that only the Klan was preventing a tide of immigrants from overwhelming American civilization on the East Coast.[87]

In the fall of 1923, one thousand Klansmen gathered in a mowed field twenty miles west of Grand Forks to listen to Ambrose speak and to install a second "club" at Larimore. With great fanfare, three hundred carloads of Klansmen arrived to watch the dramatic ceremonies. Three crosses burned. Flames blazed high as Ambrose spoke with enthused fervor on the Klan's patriotism and high ideals.

Once Grand Forks Klan reached five hundred members, it began to exert influences in local civic politics. School board members and school issues became targets. Bible reading in the public school was restored, as it had been abandoned. It was the goal of the Ku Klux Klan to crush the influences of the parochial schools.

Ambrose welded increasing power in local civic issues. In the Grand Forks city election in 1924, one Klan candidate won a seat on the city commission. Then a Klansman defeated the incumbent city justice, who was Catholic. In 1926, the Klan captured four of five seats on the Grand Forks City Commission. Once in power, the Klan decided to "clean house" of the Catholic employees. Those fired were the fire chief, with thirty-three years in the department; the city treasurer, with twenty-four years of service; the city electrician, with twenty-eight years of service; the police chief; the city engineer; the city assessor; and even the city hall janitor.

Meanwhile, the KKK was expanding throughout North Dakota. The "Invisible Empire" once drew a crowd of eight thousand in Fargo along with a parade of eight hundred robed marchers. Some on horseback, they intentionally filed past St. Mary's Cathedral on Seventh Street North. Besides a marching band and drum corps, robed children rode on a float followed by a float celebrating a little red schoolhouse. The "little red schoolhouse" was a symbol representing the Klan's support for public schools in opposition to Catholic parochial schools.

In Bismarck, at Falconers Hill, crosses burned at Klan outdoor meetings. Large Klan rallies burned crosses at meetings on the prairies between Gladstone and Dickinson and at Mill Hill in Jamestown.

And finally, Jerry Bacon, the publisher of the *Grand Forks Herald* and former ally of the Reverend F. Halsey Ambrose, saw that Ambrose had gone too far. From then on, Bacon's paper opposed Ambrose.

Scandal ripped at the national Klan scions. Hypocrisy on many levels soon caused the Klan to decline in presence and power. On November 15, 1931, Reverend Ambrose left Grand Forks to accept a call to the Merriam Park Presbyterian Church in St. Paul. Then after less than three years, he moved to Clinton, Iowa, and by 1937, he had left pastoral ministry, possibly defrocked, to enter the brokerage business. He died on December 3, 1944.[88]

The stellular rise of Reverend F. Halsey Ambrose in Grand Forks influenced much of North Dakota. His powerful orations and leadership spurred and legitimized the proliferation of the Invisible Empire throughout this rural state. However, his feet were planted in intolerance, prejudice and hatred, all coated under good intentions, and his ultimate demise signaled the end of a viable Ku Klux Klan in North Dakota.

14

TENETS OF KKK REVISITED

SEEDS IN PSYCHOLOGY
AND RELIGION

The root reasons why and how the KKK—phoenix-like—appeared in South Dakota and in the nation in the Second Klan Era are multifaceted. John Moffatt Mecklin's *Ku Klux Klan: The Study of an American Mind* (1924) describes Klansmen as frustrated and resentful because of poor conditions in their rural life. Other reasons surfaced. Disenfranchisement for white men came about because of their status in light of societal changes. New racial and religious diversity erupted in the nation. The Roaring Twenties began to roar. The women's suffrage movement came to life. New music, dances, jazz, flappers, consumerism, postwar prosperity igniting consumerism and new threats, racially and by migration, all signaled a revolution. In this mix, white supremacy blossomed, growing out of an already existing American populism. Anger, fear, frustration, hatred, disenfranchisement, the perceived need for law-and-order action and many other motivations spurred citizens to join the Ku Klux Klan. Scapegoats—aliens, Jews, Catholics, nonwhites—became handy targets. Pathological anger and frustration became contagious. All this morphed into the KKK's social platform in the 1920s, giving allegiance to Protestantism, nationalism and white supremacy.

Some South Dakotans, however, simply joined the KKK because of their need to belong to a fraternal organization. Most fraternal and civic organizations promised to provide not only companionship but also a sense of purpose. On the other hand, many South Dakotan and other American citizens chose not to join.

A deadly dance waltzed in. The Klan fostered a love fest between religion and patriotism. "Old Glory" and Christian Protestantism joined hands and heart. It emerged in an unholy marriage. For orthodox Christians and typical American citizens, it was a chilling sight to see robed figures prostrated on the ground in front of altars displaying the Bible, a cross and an American flag. The mixing together of Protestant Christianity and patriotism into one batch of dough appeared harmless—its end results, however, were deadly harmful. It was like mixing a box of cake with a can of soup. The result—"caoup." Or like the "jackalope" from Wall Drug—neither rabbit nor antelope. It became "civil religion" alive—appearing benign but ultimately corrosive.

For the Klan, however, the flag and the cross were artifacts of both religious faith and devotion to the nation. They sang, preached and lectured "The Starry Flag and the Fiery Cross Shall Not Fail." For the Klan, Protestant Christianity created a peculiar new nationalism.

The leaders of the Klan in speech and in print loved euphemisms, metaphors and allegories that promoted this "unholy" marriage. Second Imperial Wizard Dr. H.W. Evans pontificated, "As the Star of Bethlehem

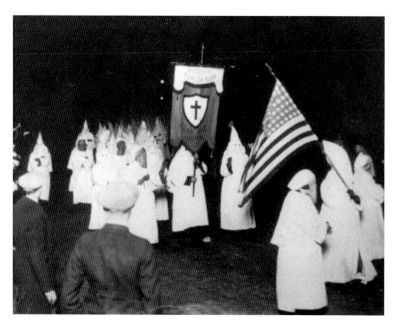

"Ku Klux Klan parade in Indiana wearing traditional KKK regalia and carrying both the American flag and the KKK flag." *Digital Public Library of America, https://dp.la/item/0a8f20360f2f479868650de31aefec42.*

guided the wise men to Christ, so it is that the Klan is expected more and more to guide men to the right life under the banner of Christ."[89]

"The real interpretation of the message of the angels who announced the birth of the Christ Child…nearly three thousand years ago, was carried forth by the Klansmen and Klanswomen of the Altoona on the eve of Christmas day, and the lamp of happiness was lighted in more than fifty homes of the poor of the city and vicinity after the Ku Klux Klaus paid his visit to the said homes."[90]

Imperial Wizard Evans believed the reborn Klan had become the incarnation of the second Protestant Reformation. In a speech he said, "The angels that have anxiously watched the Reformation from its beginning must have hovered about Stone Mountain Thanksgiving night, 1915, and shouted Hosannas to the Highest Heaven."[91]

Evans believed that the Klan had the potential to reform Christianity like how Martin Luther and the Reformers had "saved" the church back in 1517 in Germany and Europe. "The Klan crafted its own form of Protestantism, which highlighted dissent (protest), individualism, militancy and a strong commitment to the works of Jesus."[92]

Seven "sacred" symbols formed the lifeblood of the newly reborn Ku Klux Klan of the 1920s: the Holy Bible, fiery cross, flying the American flag, sword, water, robe and mask/hood. Here follow details of these and other symbols the Klan appropriated:

THE BIBLE | Protestant Bible, not the Catholic/apocrypha or seventy-three-book canon (Protestant's sixty-six books)

FIERY CROSS | Signified that the fire burned our sins and Christ is the Light of the World

STARRY FLAG | The *Kourier*, a Klan paper, reported that the flag was a "gift from the forefathers…the 'Glorious Banner' connoted both liberty and law, and yet…Old Glory was denigrated by ignorance of both."

Red equaled devotion, which might have required the "shedding of blood shed for our freedom." The *Kourier* further printed, "We love Jesus because He shed His blood for us, and we love the flag because it represents the blood shed for our freedom." The white in the flag signifies purity, intelligence and citizenship. The stars in the field of blue no longer indicate a commitment to the union but instead the realm of the metaphysical. Stars "stand for Him who is back of the stars in Heaven."

When a man turns his back on God, he turns his back on the flag. Thus the flag as a banner connotes not only American history but also the relationship of God to the American nation.[93]

ROBE/HOOD | The average Klansman's uniform consisted of a belted white robe with a cross insignia located at the left breast. The cross insignia displayed a white cross with a single red symbol in the shape of a comma. The comma actually represented a drop of blood—blood represented the blood Christ shed for all humanity. Now the robe represented the righteousness of Christ and the importance of Klan members to follow Christ's self-sacrifice for humanity.

Blood drop cross insignia depicting Christ's blood embossed on Ku Klux Klan regalia. *By KAMiKAZOW via https://creativecommons.org/ licenses/by-sa/3.0/deed.en.*

The hood, also white, covering the identity of the wearer, represented purity.

In the First Era of the Klan, the conical design supposedly imitated the ghosts of the Confederate dead. In the Second Era of the KKK, the hood's purity stood for racial and spiritual righteousness. The hood/mask hid the self so the Klansman might be unselfish in serving others. The white color also stood for Caucasian, Protestant and "native born."

BAPTISM (REPURPOSED) | Henry Peck Fry, a former Klansman, quit the Klan, revolted by the imitation of the naturalization ceremony to Christian baptism. The ceremony usurped and denigrated true Christian baptism, he declared.

The following demonstrates the false rendition of baptism:

"The Exalted Cyclops raises a glass of water and 'dedicates' the alien, setting him apart from the men of his daily association.…He is then caused to kneel upon his right knee, and a parody of the beautiful hymn 'Just as I am Without One Plea,' is sung by those of the elect who can carry a tune.…When the singing is concluded, The Exalted Cyclops advances to the candidate and after dedicating him further, pours water on his shoulder, his head, throws a few drops in the air, making his dedication 'in body,' 'in spirit' and 'in life.'"[94]

JESUS | The Klan's Jesus was a "Jesus" of the Klan's own making. Texas Klan member and minister W.C. Wright wrote, "We desire to call attention to some of the outstanding characteristics of His [Jesus's] life, as they pertain to the fundamental principles of Klankraft and the development of a *real, dependable character.*"

In the national Klan paper *NightHawk,* Wright pointed out Jesus had an exemplary character and that Jesus's experiences could relate to the ordinary Klansman. Klansmen could emulate his behaviors and principles for the betterment of themselves and for the good of the order. After all, "Jesus was a Klansman...a member of the oldest Klan in existence—the Jewish theocracy."[95]

Klan skeptic W.C. Witcher of Texas created a pamphlet exposing the hypocrisies and scams of the Klan. He suggested that the Klan would be rebuked rather than accepted by Jesus and that the Imperial Wizard, of the Invisible Empire, was the "Ruler of Darkness."[96]

To be a citizen and a Protestant was to be masculine, exemplifying the true Klansmen. Emulation of the "manly" Christ in self-sacrifice—the highest ideal.

SALVATION | The Klan plan of salvation is based on moral character. Its slogan was "Non Silba Sed Anthar," that is, "Not for Self but for Others."

THE LITTLE RED SCHOOLHOUSE | A symbol often seen in parades and displays represented the Klan's support of the public school system. The Klan's opposition to Roman Catholic parochial schools was based on the unfounded fear that parochial schools were a way for the pope to influence, infiltrate and control American society.

Four sub-tenets flesh out scaffolding for the KKK organization: the Ku Klux Klan is a white man's organization, a Gentile organization, an American organization and a Protestant organization.

On a propaganda poster under the title "Knights of the Ku Klux Klan—What the Organization Is—What It Stands For" is a statement that in part relates:

> *Klansmen are: Pro-American, Pro-Gentile, Pro-White and Pro-testant. The Knights of the Ku Klux Klan is an organization of Native-Born Americans, White Gentiles, Protestant Citizens formed to oppose by all legal means, every lawless element in our country: Klansmen claim the right as American, Protestant Citizens to band themselves together to perpetuate the ideals handed down to them by their American, Protestant forefathers who drafted the constitution of our Country.*

135

Investigate and find out for yourselves the type of individuals and the character of the organization opposing the Ku Klux Klan.

You will find every bootlegger, blindpigger, dive and resort keeper, every dope seller, every crook and criminal in the Unite States individually and collectively opposed to the Ku Klux Klan, and lined up with these opponents of the Ku Klux Klan will be will be found every anarchist, every I.W.W., every "Red" radical, every enemy of the public schools, every servant of a foreign Pope and every alien enemy of our country. Remember, the statement continues, Klansmen are not red, radicals, arson, thugs and murderers. They are loyal American citizens, your own neighbors, the friends you meet and are glad to greet every day. Klansmen eat at your table, regularly transact business with you and attend church with you. Klansmen are honored men in the communities in which they reside.[97]

The Klan saw themselves as law-and-order saviors. Their refrains chirped annoyingly that law enforcement was lax, especially as it related to the enforcement of Prohibition. When Edward Louis Senn, appointed U.S. Prohibition administrator for South Dakota in 1925, regularly criticized local sheriffs, the Klan gloated. Senn advised voters to oust from office what he called "rogue sheriffs."

Senn also chastised community police forces. He told an *Argus Leader* reporter in 1926 that "radical changes are necessary in police forces in seven cities in the state." Often Senn was seen as a pain, but it was true that some officers who swore to uphold the law were lax, especially with proper attention paid to the moonshiners and multiple stills in their community.[98]

The tendency to look the other way or simply "wink" at lawbreakers, eroded confidence in the minds of the public while emboldening the Klan.

The Klan championed themselves as "morality policemen." A puritanical and dated environment in South Dakota gave space and opportunity to the Klan's morality movement. Laws, some obviously archaic, on the books required no Sunday liquor sales; no prostitution in covered wagons; no Sunday baseball games, motion pictures or patronizing unlicensed pool halls; no spooning in automobiles or "neckers" in Sioux Falls city parks were to be allowed.

"Daisy Douglas Barr, a Klan poetess, wrote that the Klan was 'more than uncouth robe and hood'; it was the 'soul of America.' The Klan was represented as savior and soul of the nation."[99]

The house of America would be swept clean, and the Klan broom and mop pail would do it.

15

CHURCHES AND KKK COMPLICITY

It was an evening in 1927 at Bangor, Maine, when several Klansmen, robed and masked, interrupted the revival service of the famed evangelist Billy Sunday. The bold interrupters presented a sum of money to the evangelist and then quietly departed. Likewise, at a revival in Indiana, twelve robed and masked Klansmen interrupted the service. They marched in and delivering a gift of $50 and a special letter to Billy Sunday. The letter praised Sunday's efforts to promote Christianity in his revivals ($50 equals $870 in 2024).

Billy Sunday was a celebrity. His bombastic preaching and stage dramatics, even smashing chairs to make a point, left the audience spellbound. Many walked the sawdust trail to the front to receive Christ as Lord and Savior.

Earlier in 1886, converted to Christ, Billy Sunday felt called to preach. As he pranced, cavorted and pretended to slide into home base on stage (earlier he played on three baseball teams, often stealing bases), he preached twenty thousand sermons converting thousands. "I'm against sin, he once expounded, "I'll kick it as long as I have a foot. I'll fight it as long as I have a fist. I'll butt it as long as I have a head. I'll bite it as long as I've got a tooth. And when I'm old and fistless and toothless, I'll gum it till I go home to Glory and it goes home to perdition." Powerful evangelist. Showman. Billy Sunday conducted revivals over a period from 1886 to 1935 to increasingly large crowds.

The Ku Klux Klan's unannounced appearances did not go unnoticed. Homer Rodeheaver, Billy Sunday's music director, said, "He did not believe

Evangelist Billy Sunday demonstrates his preaching prowess and dramatic antics on the steps of the White House in 1922. Billy Sunday was the most influential American evangelist during the first two decades of the twentieth century. He preached fundamentalist doctrines as biblical inerrancy, the virgin birth, substitutionary atonement, the resurrection, heaven, hell and the soon second coming of Christ. He opposed lax morality and "worldliness." *Library of Congress Prints and Photographs Division, digital ID – NPCC. 05806.*

that any organization that marched beyond the Cross of Christ and the American Flag could be anything but a power for good."

Yet Billy Sunday responded to the praise letter, "I am not a member of the Ku Klux Klan, nor am I a member of any secret order but I have learned more tonight than I ever knew."[100]

Church service visitations by robed Klansmen became common in South Dakota. The following stories are representative of scores of church and pastoral complicities with the Klan.

The Klan paper *Dakota Kourier* from Spencer reported on March 11, 1925:

ROBED KLANSMEN AT CHURCH SERVICE
Leave Envelopes with Substantial Contribution for Pastor

Spearfish, S.D.,—A recent Sunday evening service of the local Methodist church was attended by a band of thirty robed Klansmen who at the conclusion of the opening song, took positions before the altar where their leader briefly explained the principles of the order, especially with regard to the Protestant churches of America. They then presented a sum of money to the pastor. When the collection was taken a large number of envelopes marked "K.K.K." personal for the pastor were placed in the plates. There were over 500 present at the service, and the pastor noted that the "spirit of Christian brotherhood was very evident."

When the KKK entered a community in South Dakota, its method for getting a "foot in the door" was to go to the local Protestant clergy. A pastor would be urged to accept free membership in the Klan and to become an officer of the local Klan. Nationwide, hundreds did.

This strategy of befriending the local minister was followed by asking about what was worrying the community and what its needs were. The Klan would be the solution.

Many pastors even abandoned their flocks to become full-time lecturers and organizers for the Klan.

Church service visitations became a common strategy for visibility and as an attempt to show goodwill. The robed philanthropists were encouraged by the Imperial Palace to make such offerings to ensure support of the Klan in each individual community.

WEBSTER

*The Methodist Episcopal Church Sunday evening was attended by about
25 members of the Ku Klux Klan in full regalia.*

*One of the members in a few well chosen remarks presented to the church
a beautiful silk US flag as a mark of respect to B.D. Fish, only surviving
veteran of the Civil War in our city, a member of this church. He also
presented to the church a substantial sum of money for it's kindly attitude
toward the Klan. The address by Rev. Bullock, "100 percent American,
who are they?" was an able effort and much appreciated by the large
audience. Appropriate music added much to a very fine program.* [101]

SIOUX FALLS

On November 18, 1924, just as Reverend P.G. Dennis at the First Christian
Church prepared to deliver a sermon on the theme "Who Are These Arrayed
in White Robes?" strangers robed in white marched into the church nave
and presented an American flag to the pastor. It was presented in the name
of the Ku Klux Klan.

The *Argus Leader*'s June 16, 1924 edition published this story:

*MORE THAN 100 ATTEND VESPER SERVICES—More than 100 persons
attended vesper services given under the auspices of the Ku Klux Klan on
a farm three-fourths of a mile beyond the Cherry Rock bridge late Sunday
afternoon. A sermon was delivered by Rev. Leslie Rogers, pastor of the
Emmanuel Baptist church. His sermon was an appeal for Christian living
and contained no references to the Klan or its program. The Klan Kiegle
[sic], head organizer for the state presided. He also led in the singing of
"Nearer My God to Thee."*

*At the conclusion of the sermon he spoke a prayer and announced
that services would again be held there two weeks hence, and possibly
next Sunday.*

ABERDEEN

At First Baptist Church, on April 28, 1924, Reverend A.B. Claypoole chose to speak on the topic of the Ku Klux Klan. Claypoole announced that it was not his intention to either denounce or uphold the Klan. Then he proceeded to read every article of the Klan creed from first to last. In concluding his address, Reverend Claypoole stated that if the Klan lived up to the pledges and purposes of the organization he himself was unqualified for the Klan.

STICKNEY

"One recent Sunday evening," a Klan paper reported, "four robed Klansmen attended the U.B. Church walking up to the front and quietly taking seats, remaining there through the service. During the winter, the Stickney Klan has been holding regular meetings and all of them new members have been taken into the organization....The good people of Stickney are all glad of the fact that the Klan appear to be welcomed."

REDFIELD

On October 27, 1924, the *Mitchell Daily Republic* reported:

KLANS MARCH INTO CHURCH SILENTLY AND LEAVE PASTOR MONEY

Redfield Oct. 27—People in the congregation at the Congregational Church were surprised last Sunday evening when at the conclusion of the preaching service, four men in the robes of the Klan marched into the church and left a packet with Rev. Samuel Johnson. Not a word was spoken and the men marched out as quietly as they came. Their gift was a check to cover part of the expense of the presentation of the picture "The Spirit of the U.S.A." which was shown that evening.

The *Mitchell Daily Republic* also reported, "On September, 29, 1924, six robed Klansmen entered the evening services at the Deadwood Baptist Church and left a sack containing ninety-six dollars. As usual, the large attendance at the church led church officials to believe that the event had been pre-arranged."

RAPID CITY

According to the *Rapid City Journal* on October 22, 1924, the Sunday evening services of the Presbyterian church were interrupted by the appearance of twelve Ku Klux Klan members who left a sack with one hundred silver dollars ($1,735.83 in 2024). The spokesman for the Klan told the Reverend James McAuley that the money was for the personal use of him and his family.

BERESFORD

The *Beresford News*, Thursday, February 7, 1924, announced, "Ku Klux Klan ideas by the Imperial Wizard of the order will be discussed at the Congregational Church Sunday evening at 7:30. Rev Hyatt announces that his lecture will be based on a printed copy of the Imperial Wizard's speech, which is being sent out through the mail of the nation. Everyone is invited to hear this discussion."

CANTON

The *Sioux Valley News* Thursday, June 4, 1923 edition carried this story:

> *A most unique service was held in the Methodist church last Sunday evening when the Ku Klux Klan presented Rev. Kearton and the M.E. Church with a beautiful flag. Rev. Kearton expressed his appreciation saying he felt the flag a necessary piece of furniture, not only in his own church, but for every public building.*

The *Sioux Valley News*, Thursday, August 2, 1923 edition carried a long essay promoting the Klan by a Reverend O.B. Preston, written while he

Congregational Church in Beresford, South Dakota, visited by members of the local Ku Klux Klan offering donations. *Author's collection.*

was vacationing in Kansas and observing the presence and activities in that state:

> *The assembly and parade of the Klan at Topeka Saturday were of such nature as to reveal many indications of both the power and the orderliness of the organization. A gathering of several thousand Klansmen of a city listed with a population of fifty-five thousand and drawing forth into the streets many thousand spectators is something to consider.... Orderliness of Klansmen and spectators throughout it all was one of the most forceful things in evidence.... The legend of the day was "a one—hundred percent Americanism."*

ROWENA

The Rowena Methodist Church was founded in 1902 soon after the town of Rowena emerged in 1888 after the opening of a nearby quartzite

Methodist Church in Rowena,
South Dakota, harassed by the
local Ku Klux Klan.
Author's collection.

mine. As part of the history of the church, two young girls held ice cream socials to raise sixty dollars for a church bell. In the 1920s, unsuccessful attempts were made by the local Ku Klux Klan to infiltrate the church. On one occasion, the KKK tolled the church bell, which was actually the community fire signal, to draw attention to a burning cross on a nearby hill.

VIBORG

The *Dakota Republic* of April 3, 1924, quoting the *Viborg Enterprise*, reported the following story:

> *A lady receiving donations for homes for orphaned children or something to that effect was in Viborg last Friday and at the same time took the opportunity to distribute several magazines, some of which were very much in favor of the Ku Klux Klan. There was especially one article that stated the K.K.K. must save America. When we need an organization of this sort to save our country, things have sure come to a pretty pass.*—Viborg Enterprise

GAYVILLE / VOLIN

A pro-KKK sermon was preached in Gayville by Reverend C.E. Stuck at the Methodist church and published in the *Volin Advance* in March 1924. Selected excerpts follow:

> *Text: Romans 12:10 "Be ye kindly affectionate one to another with brotherly love; in honor preferring one another."*
>
> *The idea which prompted me to bring this message was not one of gaining popularity or notoriety for myself, but rather to enlighten a misguided public into the light of real intelligence.*
>
> *Go into the misty past, delve into the historical events that brought this institution which has the whole nation in it's grip. It was the lawless element that was trying to usurp the power of the South that we knew immediately after the war of '61–65, especially North Carolina.*
>
> *I have been reliably informed that in order to become a member of the Ku Klux Klan one must be native born American citizen having the best interest of your community, city, state and nation at heart: must nor owe any allegiance to any foreign government, political party, sect, creed or ruler and must be engaged in some legitimate occupation, and believe in the principles by which the organization is governed.*

In the September 27, 1923 *Argus Leader*, Reverend C. Eldon Stuck, Methodist pastor of Gayville, went on the attack in one of his regular Sunday evening services against critics of the Klan:

> *"The Ku Klux Klan is not un-American, but is serving a valuable purpose in keeping the ship of state on an even keel." After reviewing the principles which he declared the Klan stood for including the tenets of the Christian religion, white supremacy, protection of pure womanhood, just laws and liberty, free public schools, free press and speech, sovereignty of state rights, limitation of foreign immigration, and local reforms. Stuck went on to preach… "It stands for one flag, one Bible, one God, Call it un-American if you will. It is not anti-jew, anti-Catholic, or anti-negro. It is pro-American first, last, and always, and my God's blessing rest upon this congregation if the things outlined here are true and I have every reason to believe they are."*

An *Edmunds County Democrat* editorial responded to Stuck's sermon, saying, "The Ku Klux Klan does not become permeated with the odor of sanctity simply because some foolish and fanatical preacher gets up in his pulpit every once in a while and makes a mockery of the religion of Jesus Christ by praising the Klan."

The *Dakota Republican* on March 13, 1924, headlined:

PASTOR RESIGNS WHEN KLAN TALK RULED OUT
Volin Methodists Don't Want Any Ku Kluxers Orating from Their Church Pulpit

Rev Stuck, last week, advertised in the Volin Advance *that his Sunday night sermon subject would be "Who, What and Why is the Ku Klux Klan." When the members of the official board read the notice they decided to request Rev. Stuck not to discuss the Klan in the church pulpit.*

In his resignation after the morning service, Reverend Stuck held that he did not permit the board to pick his sermon subjects. At this time, a cross burned near the home of another Volin minister, Reverend L.O. Sunde.

The connection remained unclear. Reverend Sunde, whose inclinations were in favor of the Ku Klux Klan, then accepted a call from St. Paul Bruel and Immanuel congregations in Union County.

In the *Beresford News* on Thursday 7, 1924, this announcement was made: "Ku Klux Klan ideas by the Imperial Wizard of the order will be discussed at the Congregational Church Sunday evening at 7:30. Rev. Hyatt announces that his lecture will be based on a printed copy of the Imperial Wizard's speech, which is being sent out through the mail of the nation. Everyone is invited to hear this discussion."

Gradually, the KKK made its presence increasingly visible by participation at funerals. The *Argus Leader* carried the following article on October 18, 1924:

FIFTY KLANSMEN ATTEND FUNERAL
Members of K.K.K., in Full Regalia, Turn Out at Huron to Honor R.B. Knight

Huron, Oct. 18—Men dressed in the white hoods and robes of the Knights of the Ku Klux Klan numbering 50 attended the funeral services of R.B. Knight here yesterday afternoon at the Congregational Church. This was the first public funeral held in Huron at which members of the "invisible empire" have appeared in regalia. Masons, Odd Fellows, Modern Woodmen and members of the railroads brotherhoods to which Mr. Knight belonged also attended the service in a body. At the grave where the Mason service were held, the Klansmen formed a circle outside the Masonic service at the grave while one of the hooded trumpeteers sounded, "Taps."

In the pages of the *Imperial Night Hawk*, the official organ of the KKK, Protestant ministers defended the Klan. A Reverend H.R. Gebhart of Indiana spouted,

God is surely with the Knights of the Ku Klux Klan....I can see the hand of God more and more in this movement....The Protestant churches have lacked unity, but through this wonderful movement they are becoming united in a common cause. All I can say is: Thank God for the Knights of the Ku Klux Klan.[102]

One purpose of this book is to "strengthen our democracy" by highlighting and reaffirming the democratic principle of the separation of church and state. Therefore, the mixing of patriotic and religious activities was clearly lost or ignored in the 1920s Ku Klux Klan movement.

Today, as this is being written, there is a surge and a movement called Christian Nationalism in the United States. This unholy marriage between right-wing evangelicals and political action and preferences clearly reflects a violation of the separation of church/state principle. In every age there is a call to vigilance to recall history (1920s) lest we repeat past follies.

16

CHAMPIONS FOR DEMOCRACY

EDITORS, PASTORS AND POLITICIANS

Prophetic voices began to thunder across the Dakota prairies, hills and hamlets objecting to the machinations and influences of the KKK. One voice was that of Dr. Ethelburt C. Woodburn, president of the Spearfish Normal School in 1925. Dr. Woodburn delivered a provocative sermon at the ten o'clock chapel hour against the Ku Klux Klan. By then, a local fraternity of the KKK had been formed by a group of college students and had gained a substantial membership. According to an interview Chuck Rainbow conducted with Richard B. Williams of the Sturgis school system on October 23, 1971, "a number of young men of the fraternity took exception to his [Dr. Woodburn's] comments." "They went out one night to Dr. Woodburn's garage, borrowed gasoline from his own car, and set a flaming cross in his front yard. Only the fast thinking on the part of neighbors kept his house from burning."

Dr. Woodburn had made his point and refrained from delivering more incendiary chapel talks against the KKK. Woodburn served as president of the Spearfish Normal School from 1918 to 1942. The school would eventually evolve into Black Hills State University.

The editor of the Edmunds County *Chamberlain Democrat* said in an editorial,

"Sow the Wind, Reap the Whirlwind" blasted the surreptitious organization. *"The Ku Klux Klan is just as indefensible as the mobbers are. An organization that is lawless must not whimper at the fruit of it's own folly....The Ku Klux Klan is founded on cruelty and intolerance despite all it's high sounding platitudes and pretentions, though it may still number in it's*

ranks well-meaning men who think they are doing God's work. The Puritans of Salem thought they were doing God's work when they burned "witches." The medieval Christians thought they were doing God's work when they tortured dissenters on the rack. We know now they were mistaken. In this age of reason men ought to get away from fanaticism and bigotry, and not permit their racial or prejudices to blind them to justice and charity....Masks and hoods are the regalia of cowards and evil-doers; manly men should scorn them....So long as the Klan clings to it's maskings and mummeries, it's propaganda of hate and intolerance, such as collisions and outbreaks of mob violence as have lately disgraced several cities may be expected to continue.... They are the harvests sprung from the seed the Klan has sown.

There were multiple South Dakota newspaper editors who supported the Klan, while many others did not.

On September 20, 1923, the *Pierre Capitol Journal* editorialized, "If you think there is no truth to the assertion that the Ku Klux Klan is a bad thing for a state and the nation, give a thought to Oklahoma where martial law reigns supreme and citizens live in fear of flogging and house burning without the protection of the military."

The *Doland Times Record* wrote on September 21, "If half the reports regarding the Klan are correct, the Oklahoma executive should have the moral support of the entire country. There is no room in the United States for an organization of this character." (Note: From May 31 to June 1, 1921, in Tulsa, Oklahoma, the Tulsa Race Massacre broke out, one of the worst in U.S. history. Thirty-five blocks in the thriving African American section of town known as Greenwood were burned, looted and one to three hundred white and Black citizens killed. Known as Black Wall Street, this section of town saw 1,256 houses burned as well as two newspapers, a school, church, hospital, library, stores and Black-owned businesses. Oklahoma did not escape the national plague of violence, race riots, and lynchings that scarred American life. South Dakotans, less aware of the Tulsa massacre, were spared equal volatile and destructive events—except for the horrendous treatment of our Native Americans.)

The national church press opposed the Klan. Through editorials, new stories and theological critiques, they condemned the Klan's malodorous activities. This stance reassured many Protestant church members who felt threatened by the Klan's cozy pseudo-church connections. Criticisms of the KKK burned from the vitriolic pens of most national Christian publishers like the *Christian Century*, *Christian Work* and *Christian Herald*.

When the Klan appeared to grow, the *Christian Century*'s readers were reminded that the spirit of the Klan was against the very genius of Christianity and "that if it succeeds, Christianity fails."

As early as 1921, editors, such as those of the undenominational periodical *Christian Work*, were calling for an investigation of the KKK by the Department of Justice, for the Klan was unchristian and undemocratic, promising only "deceit, delusions, hopelessness, anarchy and cruelty."

The Federal Council of Churches published two periodicals that, although not necessarily expressing the official position of the council, certainly reflected its views.[103]

Lutheran magazine called the Klan a dangerous and ill-advised scheme.

Baptists, together with Methodists and Disciples, were generally considered to have given the Klan its strongest support.[104]

Whereas many clergy joined the Klan or gave tacit support on the local level, one group did not. This group, considerable in number, came from both obscure parishes and great cathedrals. Many prominent national church leaders had both the courage and common sense to condemn the KKK.

At the Northern Methodist conference meeting in 1924, Reverend E. Stanley Jones introduced a resolution deploring Klan-like groups.

Reverend Ralph W. Sockman, senior pastor of Christ Church (United Methodist) in New York City and a prolific writer and speaker, believed that all enlightened Protestants would repudiate the Klan for its lawlessness.

Reverend Harry Emerson Fosdick, pastor at Riverside Church in Manhattan's West Village, called the Klan an "utterly un-American thing." In a 1963 letter to this author, eighty-six-year-old Fosdick, speaking to the past and present, wrote, "If I have done anything to the ministers of your era I am humbly grateful. You will need a profound Christian commitment grounded in faith, nourished by prayer and expressed courageously in service if you are to meet the world's needs."

Episcopal bishop Philip Cook issued a warning about the perniciousness of the Klan. Reverend Lynn Harold Hough, Methodist minister and former president of Northwestern University, called the Klan a "witches caldron of hatreds."[105]

Southern Presbyterian Mrs. W.C. Winsborough, superintendent of the Women's Auxiliary of the Presbyterian Church, U.S., lashed out at the Klan's secrecy, violence and doctrine of hate. Outspoken, she was not whipped for her statements, although the Kluxers were not above a little female flogging.

Harry Emerson Fosdick, influential pastor of Riverside Church in Manhattan, who along with other prominent national pastors spoke out against the Ku Klux Klan. *Encyclopedia Britannica.*

As a matter of record, ministers who denounced the Klan risked retaliation in the form of bullets, branding irons and blunt instruments.[106]

Methodist bishop Edwin Holt Hughes termed the Nordic superiority idiotic and nonsense. "It is not Anglo-Saxon blood," said Hughes, "but the blood of Jesus Christ that has made us who we are."[107]

Many South Dakota local papers likewise printed derogatory columns and opinions of the Klan, ranging from critiques of secrecy to claims of un-American and unchristian behavior.

The *Huron Evening Huronite* printed this article on April 15, 1924:

KLAN OPPOSED BY MINISTERS

Brookings, S.D., April 15—As the result of the burning crosses and the circulation of Ku Klux Klan literature in Brookings and vicinity, the Ministerial Association of Brookings at it's regular meeting this week expressed its opposition to the Klan in the following resolution: "We, the members of the Brookings Ministerial association, hereby go on record as absolutely opposed to the Ku Klux Klan organization because we stand against all efforts which create racial, religious and social prejudice, resulting in hatred, bitterness and oftentimes violence. Any organization which proposes law enforcement aside from regularly constituted civil authority, is un-American."

The *Dakota Republic* of Mitchell, South Dakota, printed an American Legion warning on February 1, 1923:

LEGION HEAD SAYS KLAN IS MENACE
Legion Wants Only Men Who Believe in their Oath to United States in Organization.

J.H. Williams, of Gettysburg, state commander of the American Legion and University graduate has issued a statement to the Legion in regard to the possible organization of the Ku Klux Klan in South Dakota, in which he declares flatly against Legion members aligning themselves with the Klan.

"It is rumored that units of the Klan have been organizing in this state," said Mr. Williams. "If that is true, there are probably some members of the Legion who belong to the Klan and who will resent this action. These men may be expected to talk against the Legion and to hinder in every way possible the membership campaign which is now in progress in the department.

For that reason it may be considered undiplomatic to present this matter at this time. I feel, however, that the loss in quantity of members that may result will mean a corresponding increase in quality: and I believe that this is a good opportunity to weed out of the Legion those men whose oath of service to the United States was merely a temporary promise made with mental reservations. The men who we want in the American Legion are men who will be as truly and unselfishly American in their ideals in time of peace as they were in time of war.

The April 3, 1924 *Dakota Republic* reprinted an article from the *Rapid City Journal* that reported the courage of one youth who dared to oppose the KKK.

RAPID CITY YOUTH SPOKE AGAINST THE KLAN GETS A WARNING LETTER

The first of the week, a youth of the city expressed in no uncertain terms his disapproval of the Ku Klux Klan to a group of Rapid City citizens who had gathered together. Yesterday afternoon the same youth found in his coat pocket a typewritten notice from the Rapid City Order, No. 5791, of the Ku Klux Klan reminding him of the occurrence and warning him to not let it happen again. The Letter was written on Klan stationery and the envelope had the name of the Klan printed across the face. The letter was a carbon copy and bore the notice, down in one corner, that a copy was sent to the Imperial Wizard. At the bottom of the letter was printed the slogan, "In union is strength."

Tom Ayres, state manager of the Non-Partisan League, pleaded for help from Governor McMaster in a telegram printed in the *Sisseton Weekly Standard* on July 8, 1921. It read in part:

I am informed that the Ku Klux Klan, a secret, oath-bound organization with a record of assassination and arson has effected an organization in South Dakota to fight the Non Partisan League. It is to be presumed, in spite of it's professions to the contrary, that it will pursue it's customary methods in the state. I demand that you protect the property and lives of South Dakota people from this criminal conspiracy against this state and use your peace officers to bring the organization of this criminal gang to justice.
Signed: Tom Aryes, State Manager Nonpartisan League.

Klan newspaper *Dakota Kourier* carried this story:

The fight against the KKK is growing more intensely and more widespread every day. And the Klan is fighting back against it's enemies with vigor. Various papers in many parts of the country says it will start libel suits against those publications that misrepresent it. In Chicago an organization called the National Unity Council has been formed with the avowed purpose of suppressing the Klan and its so called "invisible empire." The council, which is to be extended throughout the country, is headed by Edward F. Dunne, former governor of Illinois. He says the Ku Klux are a menace to the nation because they "avowedly proscribe millions of their fellow citizens solely because, either they worship God in a manner permitted by the Constitution of the United States, or because they were born without the United States." They place the black man without the pale of the law, such organizations foment racial, religious and political enmities instead of encouraging comity and friendship between all classes of American citizens, which should be the aim of every broad-minded American.

Many voices, only a whisper at first, soon became a thunderous chorus dissecting and flaying the Ku Klux Klan movement. From the lips and pens of South Dakota pundits, pastors, politicians and others who spoke with prophetic insight, the truth of democracy shone forth once again.

17
THE DEMISE OF THE KKK IN THE RUSHMORE STATE

S candal, corruption and internal discord raised havoc in the top ranks of KKK leadership in the mid-1920s. Locally, the lack of overwhelming community needs and basic hypocrisy soon drained the lifeblood from the KKK.

The Clarke/Tyler recruitment campaign was highly successful the first fifteen months. Hustlers (Kleagles) scooping up the 100,000-plus members raked in the loot, at $10 per head, adding up to over $1 million. The Clarke/Tyler team's success seemed unstoppable. Then the *New York World* newspaper began a twenty-one-day exposé of corruption and immorality in the Klan.

This disclosure by the *World* brought to light the hypocrisy of the Klan, which ostentatiously proclaimed the protection of pure white womanhood and high morals. In 1919, Clarke and Tyler were arrested while less than fully clothed and less than sober during a police raid on a brothel. They had been fined five dollars apiece for disorderly conduct. In what seemed like an attempted coverup, the page of the police docket that contained the account of their indiscretion had been removed. The scandal rocked the Klan. Clarke weakly excused himself. He was innocent. His estranged wife had instigated the raid, he claimed.[108]

But the damage was done. The field representatives were enraged. The Klan, which whiplashed men and women for misbehavior and for wrecking the foundation of the home, would have none of this behavior. The field representatives demanded that the pair—Clarke and Tyler—be fired.

Instead, Colonel Simmons dismissed the protesting field representatives. But the scandal would not go away.

Then a power struggle began in earnest. The KKK leadership changed. Master conniver and a onetime cut-rate dentist from Dallas, Hiram Wesley Evans, joined a clandestine gaggle of activists, including Tyler, Clarke and D.C. Stephenson, in a coup against Colonel William Joseph Simmons.

Simmons fell victim to a demotion to a lower "emperor" status. Eventually, he was expelled completely.

Evans gained power at the November 22, 1922 Klonvokation in Atlanta, Georgia. Dr. Evans, the Ashland, Alabama–born dentist, proudly wore the dubious crown—Imperial Wizard of the Knights of the Ku Klux Klan.

Evans's credential belied his actions. A member of the Disciples of Christ church, Free Masons, Shriners and the KKK, he led a group that kidnapped and tortured a Black bellhop after accusing the man of being involved with prostitutes in Dallas. He supported violence against minorities but discouraged vigilantism.

He promoted nativism, Protestant nationalism and white supremacy while condemning Catholicism, trade unions and communism. Evans said Jews were materialistic and resisters to assimilation while claiming not to be antisemitic.

Despite the national scandals, the Klan membership and influence grew in South Dakota. It grew in the entire Midwest, even in the middle of this hypocrisy. The highest numbers of the KKK swarmed in Indiana. Evans spoke to the Klan's largest gathering in history on July 4, 1923, in rural Indiana. Over 200,000 gathered to listen and participate. Eventually, Evans marched with 30,000 Klansmen down Pennsylvania Avenue in Washington D.C. The Klan reached an astounding estimated number of 2.5 to 6 million in the United States.

Then acrimony reared its predictable ugly head. In January 1921, Evans and a group of Grand Dragons expelled the publicist Clarke. Clarke had been critical of Evans's efforts to involve the Klan in politics.

At this time, an ambitious upstart, David Curtis Stephenson, took over leadership in a failing KKK presence in Indiana. With an eye on power and eventually the White House, he developed the strongest KKK presence in the nation in Indiana. Now as Grand Dragon, he became the new "Messiah."

A soap opera–like story began to unfold. The downward plunge of the Klan began. It accelerated by the misdeeds of the "Old Man" of the Indiana Klan, D.C. Stephenson.

Hiram Wesley Evans in his glory, August 1925. *National Photo Company Collection, Library of Congress.*

Ku Klux Klan robe and hood on display at the South Dakota Cultural Heritage Center in Pierre, South Dakota. *Author's collection.*

Stephenson liked women and whiskey. Enter Madge Oberholtzer. She was short, plumpish and no beauty queen but young, and the "Old Man" began to date her. He ordered his bodyguards to summon her to his mansion. He was drunk. Later, she charged that he forced her to drink with him. While intoxicated, Madge was hustled into Stephenson's private drawing room on a train to Chicago. On the train, he assaulted her. The following morning, the two left the train on the Indiana side. Stephenson was canny enough to know that according to the federal Mann Act, he would be liable to prosecution, as Edward Clarke had been earlier. The Mann Act dealt with the transportation of an individual for the purpose of prostitution or sexual activity.

Stephenson placed Madge in a hotel. She, pretending she wanted to go out and buy a hat, stealthy purchased poison (mercury bichloride tablets), which she consumed. Stephenson became desperate. He offered to marry her. She refused. They drove back to Indianapolis. He hid her away in the loft apartment over his garage. Finally, he drove her to her home, where, after a time, she died. Stephenson was charged with kidnapping, rape and murder. He was convicted and sent to prison for life.

When released in 1956, thirty-one years later, hardly anyone remembered who David Curtis Stephenson was or what he had been as he walked out of jail. Did he have any friends left? He had at least one for a time: Mount Rushmore sculptor Gutzon Borglum. Borglum had befriended him, supported him and corresponded with him while in prison until Borglum died on March 6, 1941.

The general public was being daily "entertained" by stories of Klan violence, beatings and lynchings. This violence was directed against an ever-growing number of critics. The critics saw the Klan as a lawless threat to themselves, their families and their dreams of what America should be.[109]

The Ku Klux Klan, which flourished in the early 1920s, collapsed like a pricked balloon and vanished from the South Dakota and American scenes. Or did it?

Ken Stewart observes in his paper "The Ku Klux Klan in South Dakota" at the Fifteenth Annual Dakota Conference in Madison (edited in 1981 by H.W. Blakely) that with the Depression (1929–39) former Klanners were becoming more concerned about keeping above water than Klan activities. The influence and presence of the Klan waned through 1927–30. Klan activities fell into limbo.

Tiana McKinney, archival staff at the Canton Public Library, discovered that the large Ku Klux Klan meeting center planned for the corner of South Cedar and Sixth Streets was not shown on any Canton city map. It was never built.

The last that was heard from the (organized) Klan in the state was in 1931. The Grand Dragon of the province of South Dakota of the Tristate Realm, J.H. Bailey of Sioux Falls, made a plea for all former members to return to the Order. Apparently, no one heard the plea. The Klan was dead by 1933. The Invisible Empire had vanished.[110]

The last gasp of the national organized Ku Klux Klan came under the watch of Imperial Wizard James Arnold Colescott. Imperial Wizard Hiram Wesley Evans resigned on June 10, 1939, and "turned the reins" over to Colescott. The Ku Klux Klan continued to bleed members. The decline continued during World War II.

The Klan's association with Nazi sympathizer organizations, such as the German American Bund, and with the 1943 Detroit Race Riot proved detrimental to the Klan's public image.

In April 1944, the IRS filed a lien for $685,305 in unpaid taxes, penalties and interest from the 1920s. The Klan officially disbanded at a final Klonvocation held in Atlanta on April 23, 1944.[111]

CURRENT RIPPLES:

In a gesture more symbolic than effective, border state Minnesota secretary of state Joan Growe dissolved the Steele County Chapter of the Ku Klux Klan in 1997.

In December 2003, a memorial was erected to the three young men murdered by the Klan in downtown Duluth, directly across the street from where the lynchings occurred.

18

THE KKK RISES AGAIN IN SHEEP'S CLOTHING

W hen Professor Charles Rambow wrote his master's thesis "The Ku Klux Klan in the 1920's: A Concentration on the Black Hills" in 1973, he stated, "The chances of such an organization gaining any strength in the locality in the future seems very remote."

Now in the 2020s, Rambow shakes his head in disbelief at what he sees. The values, attitudes and hatreds of much of the KKK are back.[112]

Rambow warns that the Ku Klux Klan has not forgotten about South Dakota. "The Klan has attempted to take over the Sturgis Motorcycle Rally on at least three different occasions that I know of. In 1987, the former Ku Klux Klan Grand Wizard, David Duke attended the rally promoting the Klan cause."[113]

In 2000, Rambow's wife, Susan Rambow, met a group of bikers at Sturgis wearing lapel pins with the letters "A-K-I-A." She inquired innocently of one biker, "What is the meaning of A-K-I-A?" He explained it represents "A Klansman I Am." Bikers wearing this pin are seen every year at the rally.

On Easter morning in 2011, homes and businesses in Hill City, South Dakota, the town known as the depot for the 1880s train from Hill City to Keystone, were blanketed with flyers titled, "What Is a Klansman"—urging people to join their order, called the "Traditionalist American Knights of the Ku Klux Klan."

Living in Custer, South Dakota, from 2000 to 2019, it jolted me and my neighbors when the KKK made its appearance in my city in an odd but surprising way.

Sturgis Black Hills classic poster, 1987. *Courtesy of Charles Rambow Collection.*

Going down the mountain road to my mailbox in 2012, I found a missile had been thrown on my driveway in the night. It was a cellophane bag with a rock inside to weigh it down. It carried a peculiar message. The flyer from the "Traditionalist American Knights of the Ku Klux Klan" boldly asked "What Is a Klansman?" In ten paragraphs, the KKK flyer outlined the purpose of a Klansman. In part, it announced,

A klansman is a person with a definite purpose in life and is unyielding in his devotion to that purpose. He has sworn to cast away his own selfish desires in order to provide the needs of others, to fight until victory against all forms of tyranny is won, to preserve our Race, Heritage, Values and True Americanism.

My neighbors in this small predominantly white community with a population of over two thousand mulled about in disbelief. Custer resident Melaine Stoneman, who is Sicangu Lakota (Rosebud Sioux), her husband and six children had been recipients of not just one Klan flyer hurled into their yard but three. Whether they targeted because they were Native American is unknown.

An article by editor Jesse Abernathy in the *Native Sun News* reported that Frank Ancona, the Imperial Wizard of the Traditionalist American Knights of the Ku Klux Klan, painted a mellow (yet deceptive) portrait of the modern KKK:

A lot of people think the Klan is going out and lynching and hanging people, and that's just a complete lie.... The KKK doesn't actively recruit Native Americans or other non-white ethnicities because of its core principle of upholding the way of life of white Americans and their families.

One Custer Klan member, I know, carries a pistol on his hip as he goes about town. Open carry, legal in permissive South Dakota, posing no apparent threat, nonetheless, intimidated some.

The Klan flyer listed Park Hills, Missouri, as its mailing address along with its rallying slogan: "Fighting today for your future tomorrow."

KKK recruitment flyers appeared in the historic McKennan Park neighborhood in Sioux Falls in September 2019.

"Save our Land, join the Klan," the flyers stated. The KKK pamphlets included lollipops in the cellophane packages. As Todd Epp's article "KKK Flyers Anger McKennan Park Residents" states, this is not the first time these KKK flyers have appeared. Similar packages were discovered at a Sioux Falls polling place last November.

A *Dakota Free Press* article on September 9, 2019, by Cory Allen Heidelberg reported,

The Klan Lollipop Guild was out and about last year, too, in Sioux Falls, littering the Queen of City of the East with their child enticements....

Typical Ku Klux Klan cellophane bag delivered at McKennan Park, Custer, Hill City and other South Dakota towns in recent years. The author received several dropped at mailbox while living in Custer from 2000 to 2019. Contents at McKennan Park were a lollipop, a rock for weight and a recruitment message. *From the* Dakota Free Press, *"Klan Tosssing Candy and Hate Around McKennan Park," by Cory Allen Heidelberger.*

The Klan does far more damage to our communities by sowing falsehood and division than do any newcomers seeking opportunity, liberty and neighborly tolerance.

Jesus relates a parable in the New Testament about a certain danger to a flock of sheep. A beguiling wolf appears clothed in sheep's clothing, fools the shepherd and threatens the lives and safety of the sheep.

The wolf is back. The Ku Klux Klan never died. The doctrines of racial hate, on the surface, seemed to disappear. But white supremacy and racism simply goes underground, hibernates for a bit and then reappears in new virulent forms. "Klansmen in their peaked white hoods and flowing white robes have paraded the streets of America ever since the post–Civil War period. At times their movement flourished, they have marched by the thousands; at other times, in thin, scraggly lines. Whatever the circumstances of the moment, the hate-filled message lives on."[114]

There are no known organized KKK Klaverns in South Dakota. There are, however, isolated individuals and lone wolfs like the pistol-packing Custer resident and small groups who espouse hatred verbiage and practices. It is shocking and confounding that so many of the KKK's prejudices and tenets are alive and well in sheep's clothing today in enlightened 2024.

Opportunists and political pundits preach 100 percent Americanism, "America First" and the themes of anti-immigration, nativism, white superiority, white supremacy, and virulent antisemitism.

According to the Southern Poverty Law Center (SPLC), there are four active hate groups in South Dakota. Compared to other states, this is, fortunately, a low number. By comparison, there are fifty-three hate groups in Florida, twenty-eight in Tennessee, twenty-four in Georgia and nine in Minnesota.

The four in South Dakota according to the Southern Poverty Law Center are:

1. Amerikaner (white nationalist)
2. Patriot Front (white nationalist)
3. Proud Boys (general hate group)
4. PzG In (Neo Nazis) in Rapid City

In 2023, the Southern Poverty Law Center labeled Moms For Liberty as an extremist hate group.

19

DEMOCRACY AND THE CONSTITUTION TODAY

The *New York World*'s devastating account of Klan brutalities in the early 1920s was too specific to be ignored. The *World* made it clear that the Klan had violated a whole series of amendments to the Constitution, especially the First, Fourth, Fifth, Sixth, Thirteenth (and Fourteenth).

The First Amendment celebrates the right of freedom of religion and freedom of speech; the Fourth protects the people "against unreasonable searches and seizures"; the Fifth and Sixth guarantee that no one shall be held without an indictment by a grand jury or punished without a fair trial. The Thirteenth Amendment, passed during the Civil War, abolished slavery and "involuntary servitude."[115]

The Fourteenth Amendment guaranteed that all persons born or naturalized in the United States are citizens of the United States.[116]

The Sacred rights of mankind are not to be rummaged for, among old parchments, or musty records. They are written, as with a sun beam in the whole volume of human nature, by the hand of the divinity itself; and can never be erased or obscured by human power. —Alexander Hamilton

At the conclusion of the Constitutional Convention, Benjamin Franklin was asked, "What have you wrought?" He answered, "A Republic, if you can keep it."

When historians remember, teach and promulgate *all* of America's history—the good, the bad and the ugly—that remembrance strengthens our treasured democracy. The good we praise. The bad, the ugly—we learn from.

Presently, a skirmish has emerged in the country and particularly in South Dakota regarding what is to be taught in our school's curriculums. Will it be a sanitized, selective version of U.S. history or *all* of history— both good and bad? Some U.S. governors, school boards and communities today fear that teaching the dark parts of history will encourage youth to hate America.

In a guest column in the *Custer County Chronicle* on April 20, 2022, Governor Kristi Noem of South Dakota wrote, "This week I signed an executive order to restrict the teaching of divisive ideologies like *Critical Race Theory* in our classrooms. These ideologies reject America's founding idea and instead teach that America was founded on racism—and that is not true." (She then applauds the granite faces on Mount Rushmore and the bronze statues of presidents on Rapid City streets.)

A rebuttal letter to the editor (*Custer Chronicle*) written by Larry Peterson of Custer, said,

> *I can understand how she* [Governor Noem] *might have overlooked Crazy Horse. In the history courses I took in high school I learned very little about the many Native American leaders who are also important part of our nation's history....I am grateful there are people now at work creating a more inclusive approach to the teaching of American history.*

When Sir Peter Lely was commissioned to paint English Statesman Oliver Cromwell's image, tradition has it, that Cromwell said, "Mr. Lely, I desire you would use all your skill to paint my picture truly like me, and not flatter me at all; but remark all these roughnesses, pimples, warts and everything as you see me, otherwise I will never pay a farthing for it."

True and honest history recorded, taught and learned embraces "warts and all." Jon Meacham, canon historian of the Washington National Cathedral, former editor at *Newsweek* and Random House and author of several books, wrote in his *The Soul of America: The Battle for Our Better Angels*: "In our finest hours, the soul of the country manifests itself in an inclination to open our arms rather than to clench our fists."

Democracy and its ideals cannot be taken for granted. Liberty, equality, self-governance, freedom of speech, freedom of assembly, freedom of religion, freedom of the press, the right to vote—these are our treasures lit by the torch of Lady Liberty—just beyond the Golden Door.

20

RETURN TO WEBSTER

W hen I return to Webster, each time I drive down main street, I must remember that in the 1920s there were respectable businessmen, farmers, local citizens, neighbors, perhaps my relatives and even clergy who, caught up in the fervor of the times, either joined, supported or tolerated the Ku Klux Klan.

The scars of the burned crosses on a prairie hill just east of town, fired on July 16, 1925, are still physical reminders that once a Konvoklation hosting five thousand people arriving in two thousand cars paraded, chanted and performed their Ku Klux Klan rituals.

I remember in later years as a young lad growing up and hearing the remnants of hatreds here and there in the everyday talk around the community. Prejudices rooted in fear and ignorance flipped about regarding Jews (who supposedly controlled the banks of America), the "gypsies" who wandered in and out of the community with thievery in mind, the "bums" who rode the trains and stopped by for handouts. Socialists and "Indians" and "fish eaters" were not to be trusted.

Then I found as Chuck Rambow did the racist postcard on the following page in our family vintage possessions. It's from one of my relatives to another in 1910. Oh my!

But we in South Dakota and beyond believed Lincoln's words: "We hold these truths to be self-evident, that all men are created equal, that they are endowed by their Creator with certain unalienable Rights, that among these are Life Liberty and the Pursuit of Happiness."

We believed that to maintain our democracy is to enable the light of truth to shine on all that we say or do. We knew that whenever truth is limited, tyranny takes root. We echoed the words in John's gospel, "You shall know the truth and the truth shall make you free."

Most importantly, I remember the positive. I remember churches in the Webster area that settled Latvian immigrant refugees and farmer neighbors conducting planting and/or harvest bees for an injured or sick farmer, a thousand homemade quilts made by ladies of congregations to be sent to missions and ecumenical prayer events in churches including Catholics. I benefited from my several pastors who preached the Gospel of Christ and not the gospel of the Klan.

Symbols of inclusion, democracy and equality are emerging in South Dakota today. Locals and tourists are educated and inspired when watching the emerging Crazy Horse monument at Custer sculpted by the inspiration and request of Chief Henry Standing Bear to former Mount Rushmore sculptor Korczak Ziolkowski. Crazy Horse is the largest monument in the world celebrating the Native American peoples and cultures. It stands, yet unfinished, as one of the eighth wonders of the world.

In September 2016, *Dignity of Earth and Sky*, a fifty-foot statue overlooking the Missouri River at Chamberlain, South Dakota, was erected. Designed

Racist postcard naively received by author's family member in 1910. *Author's collection.*

Chief Henry Standing Bear requested sculptor Korczak Ziolkowski to honor the original peoples of the land by sculpting Crazy Horse Monument in the Black Hills of South Dakota. The project continues to the present day. *Photographer unknown, Crazy Horse Memorial.*

by Dale Lamphere, its purpose is to honor the cultures of the Lakota and Dakota people. Lamphere said, "My hope is that the sculpture might serve as a symbol of respect and promise for the future." The Native woman wears a typical Native American dress of the 1850s. She holds a quilt featuring 128 stainless-steel blue diamond shapes that are designed to flutter in the wind. Her quilt symbolizes honor, respect and admiration in Native American culture.

Nationally, symbols of exclusion and inequality are being critiqued as statues representing racism and bigotry are removed from public places and sequestered in museums or replaced or eliminated.

According to the State Department of Oklahoma, for example, it has required the topic of the devastating 1921 Tulsa Race Massacre to be taught in history classes since 2000 and history books since 2009.

Top: Crazy Horse Monument, Custer, South Dakota. *Carol M. Highsmith, Library of Congress.*

Bottom: Close-up of Crazy Horse Monument. *Carol M. Highsmith, Library of Congress.*

In Southern California, a multimillion-dollar beach property taken from Black owners in the Jim Crow era is presently being returned as reparations to descendants of the original property owners.

Multiple communities throughout America are rallying together in a surge of patriotism and love for America and the Constitution by removing the symbols of racism and white supremacy. They are replacing those symbols with new ones that celebrate inclusion, tolerance and respect for all.

NOTES

Preface

1. Bartos, *New Memories*, 152.
2. Ibid.
3. Ibid.
4. Ibid.
5. Ibid., 153.

Introduction

6. Emma Lazarus, "The New Colossus," inscribed on the pedestal of the Statue of Liberty.
7. Rasmussen, *Planet You Inherit*, 24.
8. Larner, *Mount Rushmore*, 187.
9. Fourteenth Amendment to the U.S. Constitution, Section 1.

1. The Murder of Father Arthur Bartholomew Belknap

10. Rapid City Catholic Diocese, January 2000, shared archive file from Sister Celine Erk.
11 Thomas G. Ryan, PhD, great-grandnephew of Father Arthur B. Belknap, interview March 2004.
12. Ibid.
13. Charles Rambow, interview by Tim Velder, 2000.
14. Charles Rambow, interview by Arley Fadness, 2019.
15. *Lead Daily Call*, October 20,1921.
16. McDonald, "Klan and the Murder."
17. Ibid.
18. Ibid.
19. Swisher, "1921 Murder."
20. Ibid.
21. Ibid.
22. *Grant County Review* (Milbank, SD), 1920–25, https://grantcountypubliclibrary.acpreservation.com.

2. The Anti-Catholic Rant

23. "American Protective Association," Wikipedia, https://www.wikipedia.org.
24. Lingberg, "StoryTelling America."
25. Peterson, *History of the Swedes*.
26. Kinzer, *Episode in Anti-Catholicism*, 97.
27. Lauk, "You Can't Mix Wheat."
28. Dolan, *American Catholic Experience*, 201–3.
29. Rolvaag, *Peder Victorious*, 104, 175, 235–36.
30. Collins and Stoel, "Invisible Empire off the Plains," 37, 39; *Fort Pierre Times*, October 9, 1925.
31. Rambow, "Ku Klux Klan in the 1920's," 74; Higbee, "Photographer's Photographer," 59.
32. Robinson, "Rev. Bishop Thomas O'Gorman," 116; undated newspaper clipping, *Bridgewater Dakota Journal*, no file, Box Bishop Marty, CDSF.
33. Holt, *Dakota*, 25.
34. Smith, "Roman Catholic Church," 122–23; Robinson, "Religion," 132.

3. White Sheets and Hoods: A Brief History

35. Cook, *Ku Klux Klan*, 9.
36. Ibid., 12.
37. Ibid., 15.
38. Wisart, *Encyclopedia of the Great Plains*.

4. Rising from the Ashes: A Revival of the Klan

39. Cook, *Ku Klux Klan*, 37.
40. Ibid., 40.
41. Mecklin, *Ku Klux Klan*.

5. The Role and Power of the Media

42. *Grand Forks Herald*, December 1915.
43. *Chicago Examiner*, October 13, 1916.
44. Dixon, *Leopard's Spots*, chapter 19, "The Rally of the Clansmen," 150.
45. Record of Anti-Catholic Agitators (n.d.), 8–9, located in Anti-Catholic Printed Material Collection, Box 6, folder 7, University of Notre Dame Archives, Notre Dame, Ind. For more on Helen Jackson's misconduct, see *A Pseudo "Ex Nun" Thwarted* (St. Louis, MO: Central Bureau, 1921), 7–12, located in Anti-Catholic Printed Material Collection, box 5, folder 6, University, of Notre Dame Archives, Notre Dame, IN.
46. Young, "First Time the Ku Klux Klan."

7. Slithering into Sioux Falls

47. Blake, *Twelve Thousand Years*.

8. The KKK Spreads Across South Dakota

48. "Corn Palace History," Corn Palace, https://cornpalace.com.
49. *Miller Press*, September 6, 1923.
50. *Argus Leader* (Sioux Falls, SD), February 20, 1924.
51. Newspaper source unknown. Date known as March 23, 1924.
52. *Fiery Cross*, 1924.
53. *Fiery Cross*, May 28, 1924.
54. *Evening Huronite* (Huron, SD), February 22, 1924.

9. Bootlegging and the KKK in the Rushmore State

55. Smith, "Verne Miller Story."
56. Leona V. Pietz, oral history interview by Kelsea Kenzy Sutton at Parkston, South Dakota, University of South Dakota History Center, Vermillion, South Dakota.
57. Cecil, *Prohibition in South Dakota*.
58. Rambow, "Ku Klux Klan in the 1920's."
59. Cecil, *Prohibition in South Dakota*.
60. Pietz, *Memories of a Bootlegger's Daughter*.

10. The KKK in the Black Hills

61. Charles Rambow, interview with the author, October 18, 2021.
62. *Fort Pierre (SD) Times*, October 9, 1925.
63. Stewart, "Ku Klux Klan."

11. Gutzon Borglum: Member and Leader in the KKK

64. Calvin Coolidge Presidential Foundation, Coolidgefoundation.org.
65. Shaff and Shaff, *Six Wars at a Time*, 246.
66. *Atlanta Georgian*, June 14, 1914.
67. Shaff and Shaff, *Six Wars at a Time*, 150.
68. Chalmers, *Hooded Americanism*, 27.

69. Moore, *Citizen Klansmen*, 14.
70. Larner, *Mount Rushmore*, 217.
71. Letters in Library of Congress, Borglum Collection.
72. Larner, *Mount Rushmore*, 219.
73. Ibid., 221.
74. Shaff and Shaff, *Six Wars at a Time*, 215.

12. Klan Flourishes in Border States and Tristate Realm

75. Hatle, *Ku Klux Klan in Minnesota*, 34.
76. *Waseca Journal*, September 19, 1923.
77. Hatle, *Ku Klux Klan in Minnesota*, 54.
78. Schuyler, "Ku Klux Klan," 234–56.
79. Ibid.
80. Ibid., 254.
81. *Nebraska State Journal*, September 26, 1922.

13. Reverend Halsey Ambrose: Grand Forks, North Dakota

82. Torgerson Papers, George E. Hunt to Torgeson, March 31, 1919.
83. Ibid.
84. Chalmers, *Hooded Americanism*, 34. One such lecturer minister came to Grand Forks in 1926. *Grand Forks Herald*, February 15, 1926.
85. Torgerson Papers, Torgerson to George E. Hunt, March 25, 1919.
86. Harwood, "Ku Klux Klan," 309.
87. *Grand Forks Herald*, January 24, 1923.
88. Harwood, "Ku Klux Klan."

14. Tenets of KKK Revisited: Seeds in Psychology and Religion

89. Evans, "Message from the Imperial Wizard," 2.
90. "Altoona, Pa., Klans Help Santa," *Imperial Night-Hawk*, January 9, 1924.
91. Evans, "Klan Spiritual," 3.
92. Baker, *Gospel According to the Klan*, 40.

93. Ibid., 72, 73; "Patriotism," *Kourier Magazine*, July 1926, 14–15.
94. Fry, *Modern Ku Klux Klan*, 22, found in Indiana Historical Society, Indianapolis.
95. Wright, "Klansman's Criterion of Character," 2.
96. Witcher, *Unveiling of the Ku Klux Klan*, 12.
97. *Voice of the Knights of the Ku Klux Klan*, vol. 1, no. 1 (a publicity sheet issued by the Grand Forks Ku Klux Klan, February 21 1923), Ku Klux Klan file, Orin G. Libby Manuscript Collection, Dakota Room, Chester Fritz Library, University of North Dakota Grand Forks. This discourse had a large circulation throughout the North and South Dakota Provinces and their individual Klans; see also Rambow, "Ku Klux Klan in the 1920's."
98. Cecil, *Prohibition in South Dakota*, 29–34.
99. Baker, *Gospel According to the Klan*, 73.

15. Churches and KKK Complicity

100. "Ku Klux Klan Gives $50.00 to Billy Sunday," *Miami Herald*, May 18, 1922.
101. Bartos Bob, a quote from the *Reporter and Farmer*, Webster, SD.
102. "Elwood, Ind., Klan Aids Revival," *Imperial NightHawk*, February 14, 1924.

16. Champions for Democracy: Editors, Pastors and Politicians

103. Miller, "Note on the Relationship," 357–60.
104. Ibid., 362.
105. *Living Church* 69 (September 1923): 708; *New York Christian Advocate* 99 (September 1924): 1,167.
106. See, for example, accounts in *Christian Century* 16 (August 1924), 1,119–20; *New York Times*, July 14, 1924, clipping in ACLU files, vol. 254.
107. Miller, "Note on the Relationship," 368.

17. The Demise of the KKK in the Rushmore State

108. Cook, *Ku Klux Klan*, 52
109. Rambow, "Ku Klux Klan."
110. Stewart, "Ku Klux Klan," 261.
111. "James A. Colescott," Wikipedia, https://en.wikipedia.org.

18. The KKK Rises Again in Sheep's Clothing

112. Charles Rambow, interview with the author, 2019.
113. Ibid.
114. Cook, *Ku Klux Klan*, 2.

19. Democracy Today and the Constitution

115. Ibid., 52.
116. Fourteenth Amendment to the United States Constitution, Section 1.

BIBLIOGRAPHY

Books and Articles

Baker, Kelly J. *Gospel According to the Klan: The Klan's Appeal to Protestant America, 1915–1930*. Lawrence: University Press of Kansas, 2011.

Bartos, Bob. *Memories of the Millennium*. Sioux Falls, SD: Pine Hills Press, 2000.

———. *New Memories of the Millennium II*. Sioux Falls, SD: Pine Hills Press, 2002.

Blake, Bruce. *Twelve Thousand Years of Human History*. Sioux Falls, SD: Ex Machina Publishing Co., 2014.

Borglum, Mary Montgomery. *Gutzon Borglum: A Brief Sketch of His Life & Work*. Rapid City, SD: Rushmore Memorial Society. State Archives of the South Dakota Historical Society.

Carter, Robin Borglum. *Gutzon Borglum: His Life & Work*. Austin, TX: Eakin Press, 1998.

Casey, Robert J., and Mary Borglum. *Give the Man Room: The Story of Gutzon Borglum*. Indianapolis, IN: Bobbs-Merrill, 1952.

Cecil, Chuck. *Prohibition in South Dakota: Astride the White Mule.* Charleston, SC: The History Press, 2016.

Chalmers, David J. *Hooded Americanism: The History of the Ku Klux Klan.* Durham, NC: Duke University Press, 1987.

Collins, Lorraine, and Scott Stoel. "The Invisible Empire off the Plains." *South Dakota Magazine*, May/June 1995.

The Constitution of the United States with Index and the Declaration of Independence, 26th edition printed under the direction of the Joint Committee on Printing.

Cook, Fred J. *Ku Klux Klan: America's Recurring Nightmare.* Englewood Cliffs, NJ: Simon & Schuster Inc., 1980.

Craft, William and Ellen. *Running a Thousand Miles for Freedom.* Mineola, NY: Dover Publications Inc., 2014.

Dixon, Thomas, Jr. *The Clansman: An Historical Romance of the Ku Klux Klan.* Armonk, NY: M.E. Sharpe, 2001.

———. *The Leopard's Spots.* New York: Madison Press, 1905.

Dolan, Jay P. *The American Catholic Experience: A History from Colonial Times to the Present.* New York: Doubleday, 1985.

Evans, H.W. "The Klan Spiritual." *Imperial Night-Hawk*, October 22, 1924.

———. "A Message from the Imperial Wizard." *Kourier Magazine*, February 1925.

Fox, Craig. *Everyday Klansfolk: White Protestant Life & the KKK in 1920's Michigan.* East Lansing: Michigan State University Press, 2011.

Fry, Henry P. *The Modern Ku Klux Klan.* New York: Negro Universities Press, 1969.

Gordon, Linda. *The Second Coming of the KKK: The Ku Klux Klan of the 1920's and the American Political Tradition.* New York: Liveright Publishers, 2017.

Hatle, Elizabeth Dorsey. *The Ku Klux Klan in Minnesota*. Charleston, SC: The History Press, 2013.

Higbee, Paul. "A Photographer's Photographer: Rapid City's Bill Groethe Has Focused on the Black Hills for 66 Years." *South Dakota Magazine*, May/June 2005.

Holt, O.H. *Dakota: "Behold, I Show You a Delightsome Land."* Chicago: Rand, McNally, 1885.

Kinzer, Donald L. *Episode in Anti-Catholicism: The American Protective Association*. Seattle: University of Washington Press, 1964.

Larner, Jesse. *Mount Rushmore: An Icon Reconsidered*. New York: Thunder's Mouth/Press/Nation Books, 2002.

Lutholtz, William M. *D.C. Stephenson and the Ku Klux Klan in Indiana*. West Lafayette, IN: Purdue University Press, 1991.

Mecklin, John Moffett. *The Ku Klux Klan: A Study of the American Mind*. New York: Russell & Russell, 1963.

Miller, Robert Moats. "A Note on the Relationship Between the Protestant Churches and the Revived Ku Klux Klan." *Journal of Southern History* 22, no. 3 (August 1956): 357–60.

Monk, Linda R. *The Words We Live By: Your Annotated Guide to the Constitution*. New York: Hachette Books, 2004.

Moore, Leonard. *Citizen Klansmen: The Ku Klux Klan in Indiana, 1921–1928*. Chapel Hill: University of North Carolina, 1997.

Parker, Donald Dean, comp. *Denominational Histories of South Dakota*. Brookings, SD, 1964.

Pechan, Bev, and Bill Grothe. *Deadwood: 1876–1976*. Charleston, SC: Arcadia Press, 2005.

Peterson, August. *The History of the Swedes Who Settled in Clay County, South Dakota and Their Biographies.* Clay County, SD: Swedish Pioneers and Historical Society of Clay County, 1947.

Pietz, Leona V. *Memories of a Bootlegger's Daughter.* Sioux Falls, SD: Pine Hill Press, 2008.

Rasmussen, L. Larry. *The Planet You Inherit: Letters to My Grandchildren When Uncertainty's a Sure Thing.* Minneapolis, MN: Broadleaf Books, 2022.

Robinson, Doane. "Religion." In *Denominational Histories of South Dakota,* compiled by Donald Dean Parker, 132. Brookings, SD, 1964.

———. "Rev. Bishop Thomas O'Gorman, The Roman Catholic Church." In *Denominational Histories of South Dakota,* compiled by Donald Dean Parker, 116. Brookings, SD, 1964.

Rolvaag, O.E. *Peder Victorious: A Tale of the Pioneers Twenty Years Later.* Lincoln: University of Nebraska Press, 1982.

Russell, Nick. *Highway History and Back Road Mystery II.* Boulder City, NV, 2012.

Schuyler, Michael W. "The Ku Klux Klan in Nebraska, 1920–1930." *Nebraska History* 66 (1985): 234–56.

Shaff, Howard, and Audrey Shaff. *Six Wars at a Time: The Life and Times of Gutzon Borglum, Sculptor of Mount Rushmore.* Sioux Falls, SD: Center for Western Studies, 1985.

Smith, Brad. "The Verne Miller Story: From Lawman to Outlaw." *South Dakota Magazine,* May/June 1996.

Smith, George Martin. "The Roman Catholic Church." In *Denominational Histories of South Dakota,* compiled by Donald Dean Parker, 122–23. Brookings, SD, 1964.

Wisart, David J., ed. *Encyclopedia of the Great Plains.* Published by the Center for the Great Plains and the University of Nebraska, September 1, 2004.

Witcher, W.C. *The Unveiling of the Ku Klux Klan.* Fort Worth, TX: W.C. Witcher, 1922.

Wright, W.C. "A Klansman's Criterion of Character." *Imperial NightHawk,* February 6, 1924.

Websites

Baker, Kelly J. "Religion and the Rise of the Second Ku Klux Klan, 1915–1922." Readex, https://www.readex.com.

Grant County Public Library, Milbank, SD. www.grantcountylibrary.com.

Lingberg, Rick. "StoryTelling America." fyi-dakota.com.

McDonald, Thomas. L. "The Klan and the Murder of Fr. Coyle." *Weird Catholic.* July 14, 2018. https://weirdcatholic.com.

Swisher, Kaija. "The 1921 Murder of a Priest in Lead." *Black Hills Pioneer.* July 27, 2018. https://www.bhpioneer.com.

Young, Patrick. "The First Time the Ku Klux Klan Was Covered in a National Newspaper Was for a Murder Jan. 18, 1868." https://thereconstructionera.com.

Papers, Letters, Presentations

Harwood, William L. "The Ku Klux Klan In Grand Forks, North Dakota." South Dakota State Historical Society, 1971.

Hayness, Dr. E.C. Imperial Representative for North and South Dakota. "The Klan in Action." Author's collection.

Lauk, Jon. "You Can't Mix Wheat and Potatoes in the Same Bin: Anti-Catholicism in Early Dakota." South Dakota State Historical Society, 2008.

Letter from Reverend Harry Emerson Fosdick to Arley Fadness in 1963 from Rivermere Apartments, Alger Court, Bronxville, New York.

Rambow, Charles. "The Ku Klux Klan in the 1920's: A Concentration on the Black Hills." South Dakota State Historical Society, 1973.

Selected Papers of the First Nine Dakota History Conferences 1969–1977, H.W. Blakely, Editor.

Stewart, Kenneth. "The Ku Klux Klan in South Dakota." History Conference at Dakota State College, Madison, South Dakota, April 6, 1973.

Archives

Aberdeen Public Library

Center for Western Studies

Dakota Wesleyan University library, Mitchell, South Dakota. library@dwu.edu.

Library of Congress

Madison Public Library

Mitchell Area Historical Society. www.mitchellcarnegie.com.

Mitchell Public Library, Archival Data Base, Director Kevin Kenkel, Zach North, Archivist, Mitchell, South Dakota.

Siouxland Heritage Museums, Minnehaha County, Sioux Falls, SD.

South Dakota State Archives, Pierre, South Dakota. https//history.sd.gov/archives/newspaperarchive.aspx.

Southern Poverty Law Center

Watertown Public Library

ABOUT THE AUTHOR

Arley Kenneth Fadness was born and raised in the Webster, South Dakota area. His literary efforts include several historical and religious books. Among his most recent are *Capturing the Younger Brothers Gang in the Northern Plains: The Untold Story of Heroic Teen Asle Sorbel* (The History Press); *A Long, Long Road Back to Love* (CSS Publishing); *Balloons Aloft: Flying South Dakota Skies* (Xulon Press); and *Six Spiritual Needs in America Today* (CSS Publishing).

Arley is a retired draftsman and clergy. He is an active writer and presenter of history/cultural programs for the South Dakota Humanities. Arley is married to Pamela, and the couple have four adult children—Timothy, Susan, Joel and Rebekah—and one grandchild, Ela Rae.

Arley earned a doctor of ministry degree through McCormick Theological Seminary in Chicago after attending Luther Seminary, Augustana College and Pacific Lutheran College.

He served a dozen parishes, restored a 1956 Thunderbird and 1930 Model A Ford Roadster; drew ballooning blueprints for father and inventor of the modern hot air balloon, Ed Yost; and now loves outdoor concerts at the Levitt and hiking Good Earth State Park.